Elegant Needle

CONTENTS

★ Copyright © 1987, 1988 ONDORISHA PUBLISHERS LTD., All Rights Reserved
★ Published by ONDORISHA PUBLISHERS LTD., 32 Nishigoken-cho, Shinjuku-ku, Tokyo 162, Japan
★ Sole Overseas Distributor: Japan Publications Trading Co., Ltd.
  P.O. Box 5030 Tokyo International, Tokyo, Japan
★ Distributed in the United States by Kodansha International/USA, Ltd.
  through Harper & Row, Publishers, Inc., 10 East 53rd Street, New York, New York 10022
  Australia by Bookwise International, 1 Jeanes Street, Beverley, South Australia 5007, Australia

10 9 8 7 6 5 4 3 2 1

ISBN 0-87040-750-3
Printed in Japan

PART
[1]
FASHION

Picture

Design on page 2.

Picture (embroidery design)

Shown on page 1.

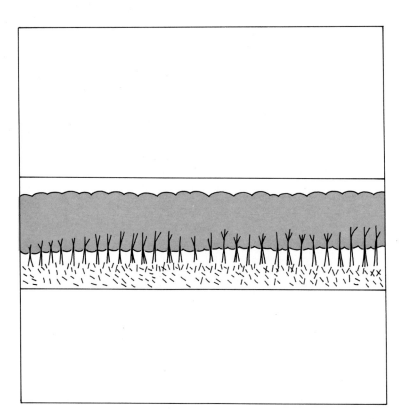

Brooches A, B, F, H, M, O & R

Shown on pages 4 & 5.

MATERIALS: Velveteen: one 14 cm by 7 cm (5¹/₂″ × 2³/₄″) piece each: Gray for *A* & *M*; Dark Gray for *B*; Blue for *H*; Peacock Green for *R*. Cotton satin one 14 cm by 7 cm (5¹/₂″ × 2³/₄″) piece each: Gray for *F*; Charcoal Gray for *O*. DMC six-strand embroidery floss, No. 25: Small amount each of Ash Gray (762) for *A, B,* & *M*; Gray (318) for *F*; Gray (414) for *O*; Antique Blue (930) for *H*; Golden Green (580) for *M*; Sky Blue (517) for *R*. Silver lamé thread for *A, B, F, H, M, O* & *R*. Black lamé thread for *B*. Round seed beads, 1.7 mm (¹/₁₆″): 48 Light Lavender and 52 Gray for *A*; 30 Silver and 19 Platinum for *B*; 52 Navy for *F*; 48 Platinum for *H*; 49 Gray for *M*; 18 Silver Gray for *O*. 47 Pearl beads, 0.2 cm (¹/₈″) in diameter for *R*. One star-shaped Gold spangle, 0.5 cm (¹/₄″) in diameter for *H*. Polyester fiberfill. Cardboard, 4.3 cm (1³/₄″) in diameter.

FINISHED SIZE: 4.3 cm (1³/₄″) in diameter.

DIRECTIONS: Transfer design onto center of fabric. Embroider and sew beads in place. Make brooches following diagrams shown on the opposite page.

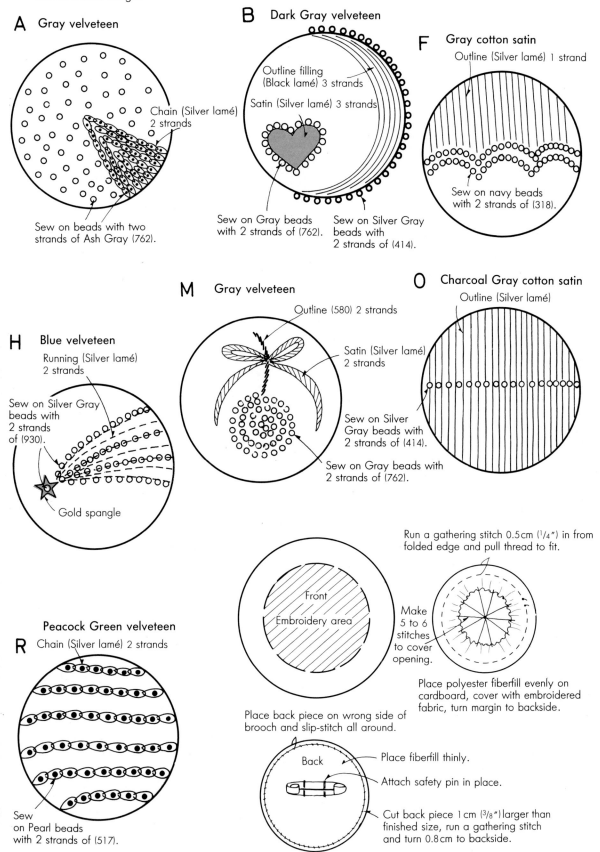

1 cm all around margin.

A Gray velveteen

Chain (Silver lamé) 2 strands

Sew on beads with two strands of Ash Gray (762).

B Dark Gray velveteen

Outline filling (Black lamé) 3 strands

Satin (Silver lamé) 3 strands

Sew on Gray beads with 2 strands of (762).

Sew on Silver Gray beads with 2 strands of (414).

F Gray cotton satin

Outline (Silver lamé) 1 strand

Sew on navy beads with 2 strands of (318).

H Blue velveteen

Running (Silver lamé) 2 strands

Sew on Silver Gray beads with 2 strands of (930).

Gold spangle

M Gray velveteen

Outline (580) 2 strands

Satin (Silver lamé) 2 strands

Sew on Silver Gray beads with 2 strands of (414).

Sew on Gray beads with 2 strands of (762).

O Charcoal Gray cotton satin

Outline (Silver lamé)

R Peacock Green velveteen

Chain (Silver lamé) 2 strands

Sew on Pearl beads with 2 strands of (517).

Front Embroidery area

Place back piece on wrong side of brooch and slip-stitch all around.

Run a gathering stitch 0.5cm (1/4") in from folded edge and pull thread to fit.

Make 5 to 6 stitches to cover opening.

Place polyester fiberfill evenly on cardboard, cover with embroidered fabric, turn margin to backside.

Back

Place fiberfill thinly.

Attach safety pin in place.

Cut back piece 1 cm (3/8") larger than finished size, run a gathering stitch and turn 0.8 cm to backside.

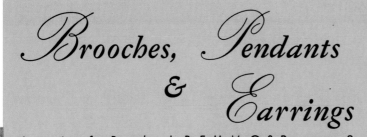

Brooches, Pendants & Earrings

Instructions for Brooches A, B, F, H, M, O & R on page 2, for I, J,L & N on page 7, for Pendants and Earrings on page 6.

Earrings D, E, K, P & Q

Shown on pages 4 & 5.

MATERIALS: Linen: Gray for D, E & K; Blue Green for Q. White cotton satin for P, one 10cm by 5cm (3⅞″ × 2″) piece each (for one pair). DMC six-strand embroidery floss, No. 25: Small amount each of Ash Gray (318) for D, E & K; White for P; Almond Green (504) for Q. White lamé thread for D. Silver lamé thread for E, K & Q. Round seed beads (1.7mm): 82 Silver for D; 40 Gray for E; 40 each of Milky White for P & Q; 68 Silver for K. 2 pieces of cardboard, 2.5cm (1″) in diameter. Polyester fiberfill. Earring clips.

FINISHED SIZE: 2.5cm (1″) in diameter.

DIRECTIONS: Embroider and sew on beads in place. Make earrings following directions for Brooches on page 3.

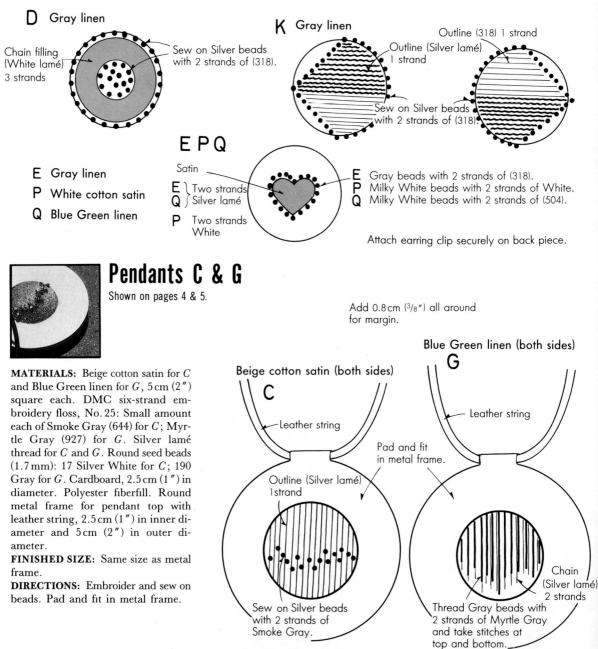

Add 0.8mm all around for margin.

D Gray linen

Chain filling (White lamé) 3 strands

Sew on Silver beads with 2 strands of (318).

K Gray linen

Outline (318) 1 strand

Outline (Silver lamé) 1 strand

Sew on Silver beads with 2 strands of (318).

E P Q

E Gray linen

P White cotton satin

Q Blue Green linen

Satin

E, Q — Two strands Silver lamé

P — Two strands White

E Gray beads with 2 strands of (318).

P Milky White beads with 2 strands of White.

Q Milky White beads with 2 strands of (504).

Attach earring clip securely on back piece.

Pendants C & G

Shown on pages 4 & 5.

MATERIALS: Beige cotton satin for C and Blue Green linen for G, 5cm (2″) square each. DMC six-strand embroidery floss, No. 25: Small amount each of Smoke Gray (644) for C; Myrtle Gray (927) for G. Silver lamé thread for C and G. Round seed beads (1.7mm): 17 Silver White for C; 190 Gray for G. Cardboard, 2.5cm (1″) in diameter. Polyester fiberfill. Round metal frame for pendant top with leather string, 2.5cm (1″) in inner diameter and 5cm (2″) in outer diameter.

FINISHED SIZE: Same size as metal frame.

DIRECTIONS: Embroider and sew on beads. Pad and fit in metal frame.

Add 0.8cm (⅜″) all around for margin.

Beige cotton satin (both sides)

C

Leather string

Outline (Silver lamé) 1 strand

Sew on Silver beads with 2 strands of Smoke Gray.

Blue Green linen (both sides)

G

Leather string

Pad and fit in metal frame.

Chain (Silver lamé) 2 strands

Thread Gray beads with 2 strands of Myrtle Gray and take stitches at top and bottom.

Brooches J & N

Shown on pages 4 & 5.

MATERIALS: Silver lamé fabric for front of *J*, Gray cotton satin for back of *J* and front of *N*, Charcoal Gray cotton satin for back of *N*, 7 cm (2⅞″) square piece each. DMC six-strand embroidery floss, No. 25: Small amount each of Ash Gray (415) for *J* and *N*. Silver lamé thread. 4 round seed beads in Silver Gray (1.7 cm or ¹/₁₆″). Ball-shaped frosted beads: 3 for *J* (0.3 cm in diameter); 4 (0.8 cm or ⅜″), 21 (0.5 cm or ¼″), 13 (0.3 cm or ⅛″), 1 Silver (0.5 cm) and 1 (0.3 cm) for *N*. Cardboard, 4.3 cm (1¾″) in diameter. Polyester fiberfill. Round metalframes for brooch, 4 cm (1⅝″) in inner diameter and 7 cm (2⅞″) in outer diameter.

FINISHED SIZE: Same size as round metal frame.

DIRECTIONS: Embroider and sew on beads. Pad and make brooches according to directions on page 3.

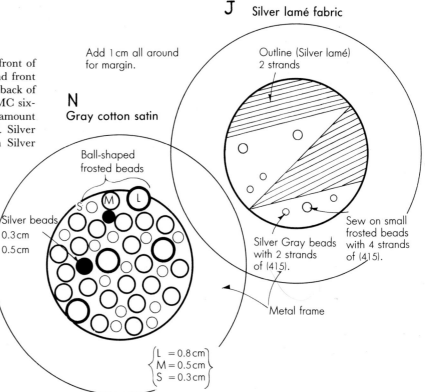

Add 1 cm all around for margin.

J Silver lamé fabric

N Gray cotton satin

Outline (Silver lamé) 2 strands

Ball-shaped frosted beads

Sew on small frosted beads with 4 strands of (415).

Silver Gray beads with 2 strands of (415).

Silver beads
0.3 cm
0.5 cm

Metal frame

L = 0.8 cm
M = 0.5 cm
S = 0.3 cm

Brooches I & L

Shown on pages 4 & 5.

MATERIALS: Cotton satin: Beige for *I* and Ash Brown for *L*, 9 cm (3½″) square piece each. DMC six-strand embroidery floss, No. 25: Small amount each of Smoke Gray (642) for *I* and Beige (3022) for *L*. Round seed beads (1.7 mm or ¹/₁₆″): 9 Bronze for *I*; 194 Silver for *L*. Tear-drop-shaped beads (0.7 cm or ¼″ long): 9 for *I*; 1 for *L*. Cardboard, 6 cm (2⅜″) in diameter. Safety pins.

FINISHED SIZE: 6 cm (2⅜″) in diameter.

DIRECTIONS: See directions on page 3.

Add 1.5 cm (⅝″) all around for margin.

I Beige cotton satin

L Ash Brown cotton satin

Chain (Smoke Gray) 3 strands

Bronze beads with 2 strands of Smoke Gray.

Chain (Beige) 2 strands

Silver beads with 2 strands of Beige.

Tear-drop-shaped bead

Tear-drop-shaped beads

Accessories for Shoes

Instructions on page 10.

Necklace and Bracelet

Instructions on page 11.

Accessories for Shoes A, B, C & D
Shown on page 8.

MATERIALS: Linen: Gray for A and C, Moss Green for B, and Brown for D, 12cm ($4^5/8''$) square each. DMC six-strand embroidery floss, No. 25: Small amount each of Almond Green (504, 524) for B; Ash Gray (318) for C and Dark Brown (3031) for D. Silver lamé thread for A. Round seed beads (1.7mm or $^1/16''$): Small amount each of Pearl Gray for A, Olive Green for B, Silver for C and Bronze for D. Cardboard, 4.5cm ($1^7/8''$) in diameter. Polyester fiberfill. Clips.

FINISHED SIZE: 4.5cm ($1^7/8''$) in diameter.

DIRECTIONS: Embroider and sew on beads in place. Make Shoes Ornaments in same manner as Brooches on page 3. Attach clip in place.

A

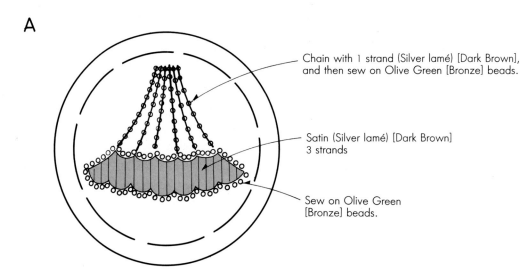

Chain with 1 strand (Silver lamé) [Dark Brown], and then sew on Olive Green [Bronze] beads.

Satin (Silver lamé) [Dark Brown] 3 strands

Sew on Olive Green [Bronze] beads.

To make C and D, use threads and beads shown in brackets.

B

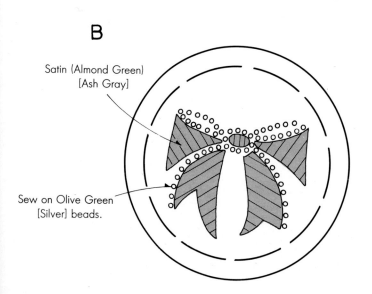

Satin (Almond Green) [Ash Gray]

Sew on Olive Green [Silver] beads.

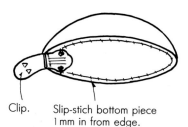

Clip.

Slip-stich bottom piece 1mm in from edge.

Sew on beads with 2 strands of thread matching embroidery.

Necklace and Bracelet

Shown on page 9.

MATERIALS: DMC embroidery thread, No. 3: $2^1/2$ skeins of Almond Green (502) for *Necklace*; small amount each of Indigo (322) and Gray (318) for *Bracelet*. DMC six-strand embroidery floss, No 25: Small amount of Almond Green (502) for *Necklace*. For *Necklace*: 33 round seed beads in Sea Green (1.7 mm or $^1/_{16}''$); 33 Navy spangles, 1.6 cm in diameter. For *Bracelet*: 15 Blue diamond-cut beads, 0.6 cm in diameter. One pair of bracelet clasps. Transparent vinyl tube, 15 cm long and 0.7 cm in diameter ($5^7/_8'' \times ^1/_4''$). Tapestry needle.
FINISHED SIZE: *Necklace*: 75 cm ($29^1/2''$) long. *Bracelet*:

22 cm ($8^5/_8''$).
DIRECTIONS: For *Necklace*: Cut embroidery thread into 27 lengths of 90 cm ($35^3/_8''$), divide them into three groups and braid. Make knot at each end. Starting at center, attach each spangle with one bead using two strands of floss. For *Bracelet*: Cut Ash Gray thread to 12 lengths and Indigo to 5 lengths, 25 cm ($9^7/_8''$) long each. Pass all thread through vinyl tube and pass 3 diamond-cut beads through three threads. Repeat this procedure four more times and end with vinyl tube. Attach clasps for bracelet at each end.

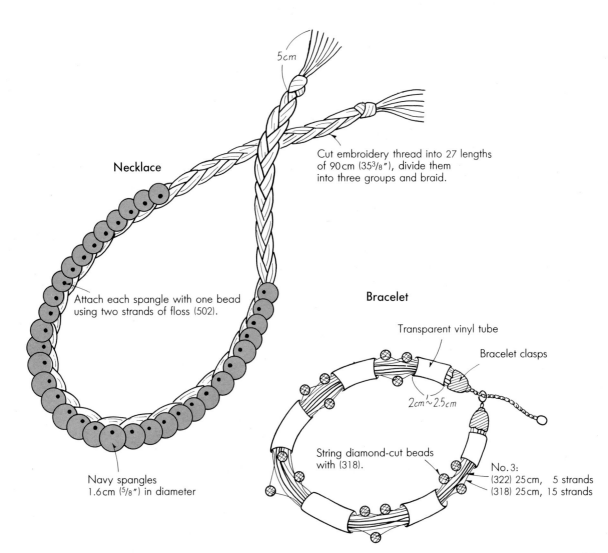

5cm

Necklace

Cut embroidery thread into 27 lengths of 90 cm (35³/₈″), divide them into three groups and braid.

Attach each spangle with one bead using two strands of floss (502).

Navy spangles 1.6 cm (⁵/₈″) in diameter

Bracelet

Transparent vinyl tube

Bracelet clasps

2cm~2.5cm

String diamond-cut beads with (318).

No. 3:
(322) 25cm, 5 strands
(318) 25cm, 15 strands

Fancy T-Shirts

Instructions for Anchor, Bow and Cat on page 14,
for Lightning on page 15 and for Hearts on page 40.

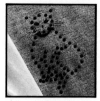

Fancy T-Shirts
Shown on pages 12 & 13.

MATERIALS: Purchased T-shirts: Dark Blue for *Anchor*, White for *Bow*, Gray for *Cat*, and Off-white for *Hearts* and *Lightning*. DMC six-strand embroidery floss, No. 25: Small amount each of Corn Flower Blue (793) for *Anchor*, White for *Bow*, Ecru for *Hearts* and *Lightning*, and Black (310) for *Cat*. Silver lamé thread. Round seed beads (1.7 mm or $^1/_{16}$″): 152 Navy and 55 Platinum for *Anchor*, 260 Platinum for *Bow*, 18 Black for *Cat* and 4 Silver for *Hearts*. 2 tear-drop-shaped beads, 0.7 cm ($^1/_4$″) long. Rhinestones, 0.3 cm ($^1/_8$″) in diameter: 38 for *Anchor*, 65 for *Bow*, 47 for *Hearts*, 72 Black for *Cat* and 110 for *Lightning*. Use transparent stones except for *Cat*.

DIRECTIONS: Transfer designs to T-shirts. Attach rhinestones to shirts with warm iron and beads with two strands of embroidery floss. Pass 18 round beads onto two strands of floss and stitch each end.

See page 40 for Heart pattern.

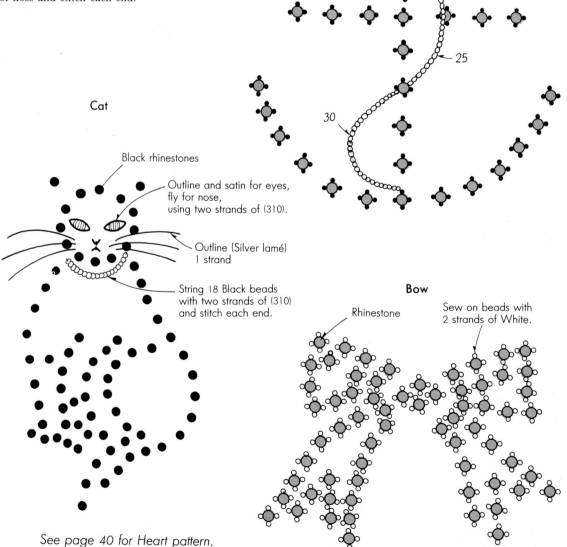

Anchor

Sew on Navy beads with 2 strands of (793).

Rhinestone

Sew on Platinum beads with 2 strands of (793).

25

30

Cat

Black rhinestones

Outline and satin for eyes, fly for nose, using two strands of (310).

Outline (Silver lamé) 1 strand

String 18 Black beads with two strands of (310) and stitch each end.

Bow

Rhinestone

Sew on beads with 2 strands of White.

Placement for Lightning

Transfer Lightning design onto T-shirt following illustration on left.
Attach rhinestones with warm iron.

Attach 110 rhinestones onto front and back.

Chic Blouse

Instructions on page 18.

Shoes Case

Instructions on page 19.

Chic Blouse

Shown on page 16.

MATERIALS: Purchased Gray blouse. DMC six-strand embroidery floss, No. 25: Half skein of Ash Gray (318).
DIRECTIONS: Transfer design onto blouse. Reverse design for right side. Embroider in satin and outline stitches with two strands of floss.

Pattern for left side

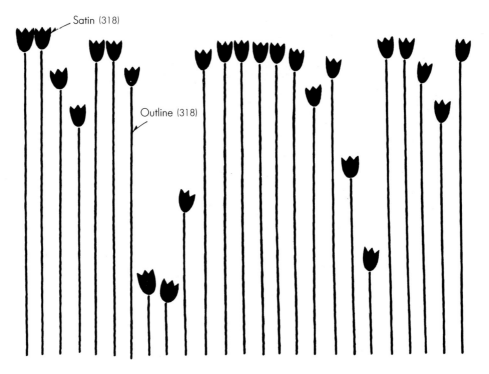

Satin (318)

Outline (318)

Use two strands of floss.

Shoes Case

Shown on page 17.

MATERIALS: Blue cotton fabric, 90 cm by 40 cm (35³⁄₈″ × 15³⁄₄″). DMC six-strand embroidery floss, No. 25: Small amount each of Beaver Gray (647), Antique Blue (931) and Green (3052). Silver lamé thread. One skein of Blue Pearl cotton, No. 4.
FINISHED SIZE: See diagram.
DIRECTIONS: Cut fabric adding seam allowance indicated in parentheses. Transfer design and embroider following illustration. Sew side seam and neaten raw edges with zigzag machine-stitch. Fold top edge twice and stitch. Sew on strip for casing. Cut Blue thread to 4 lengths of 80 cm (31¹⁄₂″) and insert into casing. Tie both ends together.

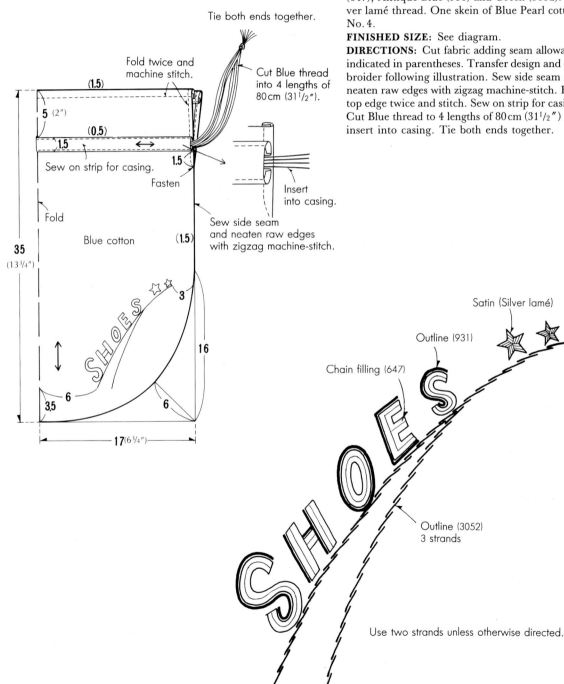

Tie both ends together.

Fold twice and machine stitch.

Cut Blue thread into 4 lengths of 80 cm (31¹⁄₂″).

(1.5)

5 (2″)

(0.5)

1.5

1.5

Sew on strip for casing.

Fasten

Insert into casing.

Fold

Blue cotton

(1.5)

Sew side seam and neaten raw edges with zigzag machine-stitch.

35 (13¹⁄₄″)

3

16

6

3.5

6

17 (6³⁄₄″)

Satin (Silver lamé)

Outline (931)

Chain filling (647)

Outline (3052)
3 strands

Use two strands unless otherwise directed.

Å

MARCH HARE

Lovely Handkerchiefs

Instructions for A & B on page 22
and for C & D on page 23.

B★

C★

D★

Lovely Handkerchiefs A & B

Shown on pages 20 & 21.

MATERIALS: Cotton handkerchiefs, 40 cm (16″) square: Gray for *A* and Pink for *B*. DMC six-strand embroidery floss, No. 25: For *A*: Small amount each of Dull Mauve (316), Almond Green (502, 522), Ash Gray (318), Antique Blue (931) and Beige (3022). For *B*: Raspberry Red (3607, 3609) and Almond Green (522, 523).

DIRECTIONS: Transfer design to handkerchief and embroider. Use two strands of floss unless otherwise directed.

Use two strands unless otherwise directed.

A

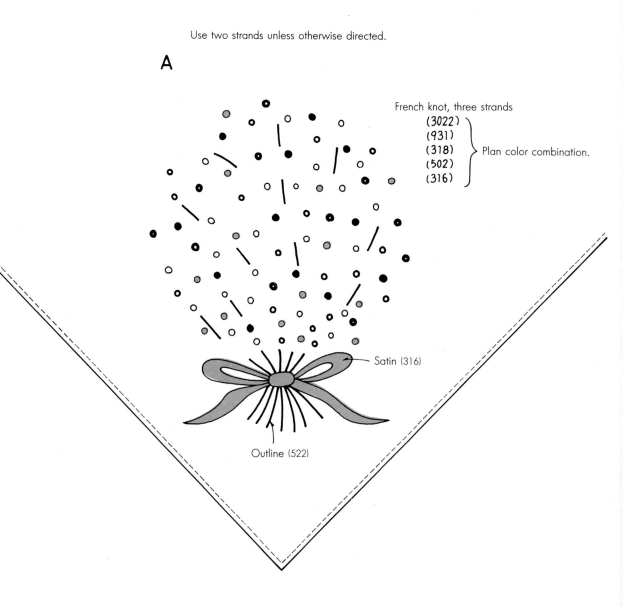

French knot, three strands
(3022)
(931)
(318) } Plan color combination.
(502)
(316)

Satin (316)

Outline (522)

Placement for Flowers

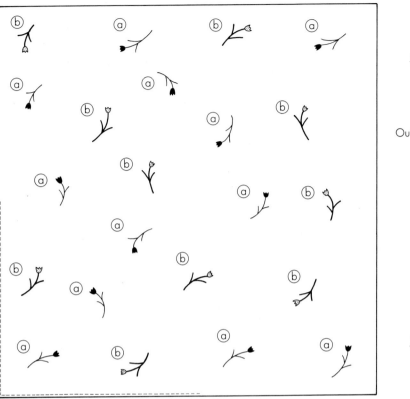

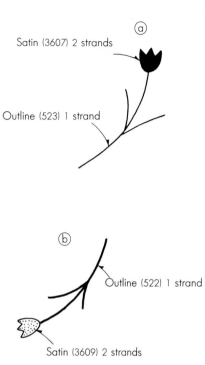

Satin (3607) 2 strands

Outline (523) 1 strand

Outline (522) 1 strand

Satin (3609) 2 strands

Lovely Handkerchiefs C & D
Shown on pages 20 & 21.

MATERIALS: Cotton handkerchiefs, 28 cm (11″) square each: Lavender for *C* and Pink for *D*. DMC six-strand embroidery floss, No. 25: for *C*: Small amount each of Almond Green (502), Mauve (340) and Moss Green (469); For *D*: Raspberry Red (3607), White and Green (3052).

DIRECTIONS: Transfer design onto handkerchief and embroider at top and bottom borders. Use colors shown in parentheses for *C* and in brackets for *D*.

Use two strands of floss.

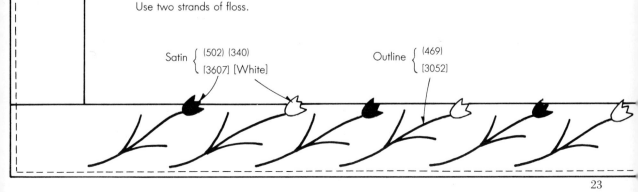

Satin { (502) (340)
{ [3607] [White]

Outline { (469)
{ [3052]

Pochettes

Instructions for Small Pochette on page 26 and
for Large Pochette on page 36.

Small Pochette

Shown on page 24.

MATERIALS: Navy linen, 45 cm by 46 cm (17³/₄″ × 18¹/₈″). Blue cotton fabric for lining, 40 cm by 20 cm (15³/₄″ × 7⁷/₈″). DMC six-strand embroidery floss, No. 25: Small amount each of Cornflower Blue (792, 793) and Peacock Green (991). Blue lamé thread. Round seed beads (1.7 mm or ¹/₁₆″): 215 Navy and 36 Dark Green. Heavyweight interfacing, 40 cm by 20 cm (15³/₄″ × 7⁷/₈″). Pearl cotton, No. 4: 1¹/₂ skeins of Green and ¹/₂ skein of Blue. Red transparent bead, 1.5 cm (⁵/₈″) in diameter.
FINISHED SIZE: 15 cm wide and 15 cm deep (5⁷/₈″ × 5⁷/₈″).

DIRECTIONS: Cut fabric adding 1 cm (³/₈″) for seam allowance. Transfer design onto back and front pieces of linen and embroider. Pin and baste front and interfacing together. Repeat for back pieces. Sew front and back together with gusset in between catching ends of tabs. Make inner case in same manner. Insert inner case into outer one, turn in top edges and slip-stitch. Attach crocheted loop at center back and sew round bead on front. Pass 15 lengths of thread into tab and tie each end.

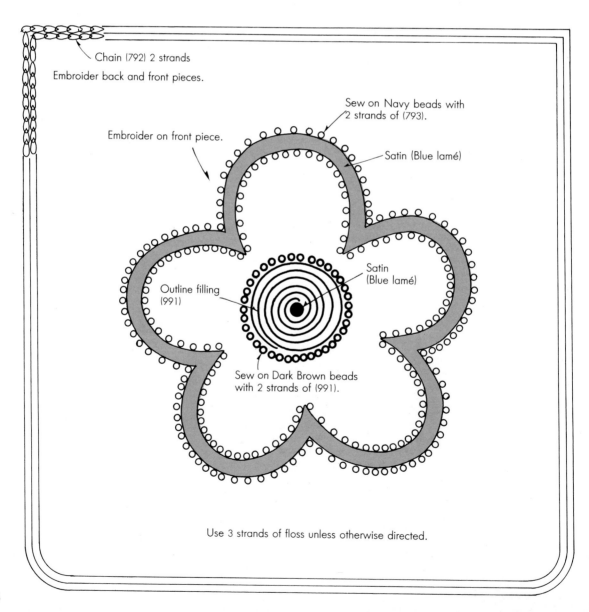

Chain (792) 2 strands
Embroider back and front pieces.

Embroider on front piece.

Sew on Navy beads with 2 strands of (793).

Satin (Blue lamé)

Satin (Blue lamé)

Outline filling (991)

Sew on Dark Brown beads with 2 strands of (991).

Use 3 strands of floss unless otherwise directed.

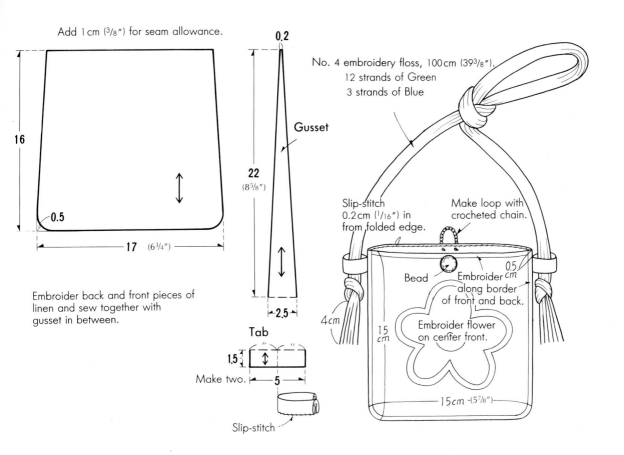

Add 1cm (³⁄₈") for seam allowance.

16

0.5

17 (6¾")

Embroider back and front pieces of linen and sew together with gusset in between.

0.2

22 (8⁵⁄₈")

Gusset

2.5

Tab

1.5

Make two. 5

Slip-stitch

No. 4 embroidery floss, 100cm (39³⁄₈").
12 strands of Green
3 strands of Blue

Slip-stitch 0.2cm (¹⁄₁₆") in from folded edge.

Make loop with crocheted chain.

Bead

0.5 cm

Embroider cm along border of front and back.

Embroider flower on center front.

4cm

15 cm

15cm (5⁷⁄₈")

Continued from page 31.

Use two strands unless otherwise directed.

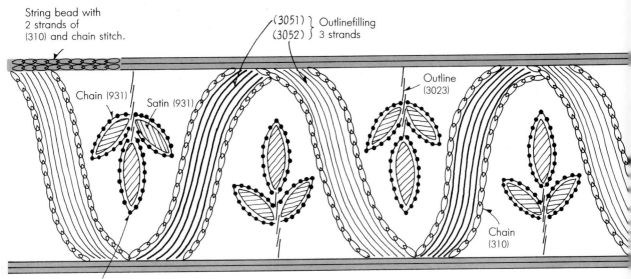

String bead with 2 strands of (310) and chain stitch.

(3051) ⎫ Outlinefilling
(3052) ⎬ 3 strands

Outline (3023)

Chain (931)

Satin (931)

Chain (310)

Sew on Blue Gray beads with two strands of (931).

Pochette

Instructions on page 30.

Sash and Matching Clutch Bag

Instructions for Sash on page 37 and for Bag on page 31.

Pochette

Shown on page 28.

MATERIALS: Black cotton satin, 20 cm by 155 cm (7⁷/₈″ × 61″). DMC six-strand embroidery floss, No. 25: Small amount each of Black (310) and matching colors with beads. Round seed beads (1.7 mm or ¹/₁₆″): 600 Black; 122 each of Olive Green, Purple, Silver, Gray, Darkish Gold, Light Lavender and Dark Silver. Ball-shaped transparent bead, 1 cm (³/₈″) in diameter. Cotton cord, 0.5 cm in diameter and 153 cm long (¹/₄″ × 60¹/₄″). Heavyweight interfacing, 30 cm by 16 cm (11³/₄″ × 6¹/₄″).

FINISHED SIZE: 12 cm wide and 15 cm deep (4³/₄″ × 5⁷/₈″).

DIRECTIONS: Transfer design onto front and embroider with beads. Sew strap, tabs and loop for button individually. Sew front and back together with gusset in between catching tabs in place. Pin and baste interfacing and lining fabric. Make inner case. Insert inner case into outer one, turn in top edges and slip-stich catching ends of loop for button. Sew on round bead. Insert each end of shoulder strap into tab and make knot.

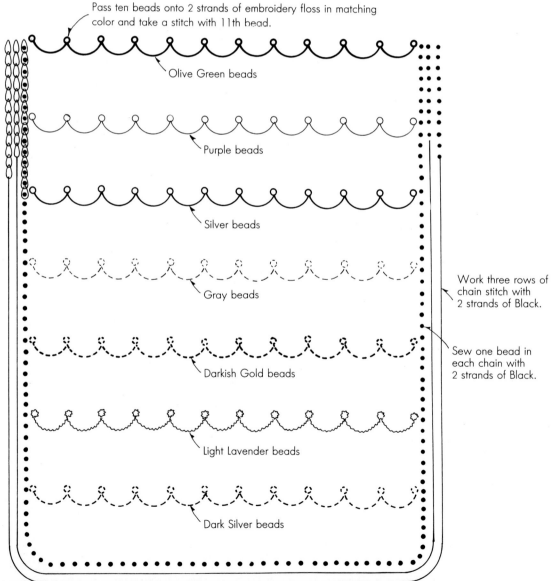

Pass ten beads onto 2 strands of embroidery floss in matching color and take a stitch with 11th bead.

Olive Green beads

Purple beads

Silver beads

Gray beads

Darkish Gold beads

Light Lavender beads

Dark Silver beads

Work three rows of chain stitch with 2 strands of Black.

Sew one bead in each chain with 2 strands of Black.

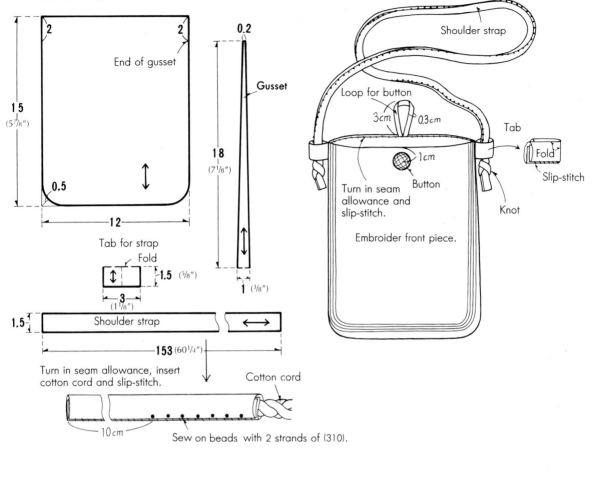

Add 0.8 cm (3/8″) for seam allowance.

2   End of gusset   2

0.2

Gusset

15 (5⅞″)

18 (7⅛″)

0.5

12

1 (3/8″)

Tab for strap

Fold

1.5 (5/8″)

3 (1⅛″)

1.5

Shoulder strap

153 (60¼″)

Turn in seam allowance, insert cotton cord and slip-stitch.

Cotton cord

10 cm

Sew on beads with 2 strands of (310).

Shoulder strap

Loop for button

3 cm   0.3 cm

1 cm

Turn in seam allowance and slip-stitch.

Button

Embroider front piece.

Tab

Fold

Slip-stitch

Knot

Clutch Bag

Shown on page 29.

MATERIALS: Black cotton satin, 90 cm by 40 cm (35⅜″ × 15¾″). DMC six-strand embroidery floss, No. 25: Small amount each of Green (3051, 3052), Antique Blue (931), Beige (3023) and Black (310). Round seed beads (1.7 mm or 1/16″): 375 Black and 322 Blue Gray.

FINISHED SIZE: 27 cm wide and 17 cm deep (10⅝″ × 6¾″).

DIRECTIONS: Cut out front piece. Transfer design in place and embroider. You may need professional help to shape and finish bag.

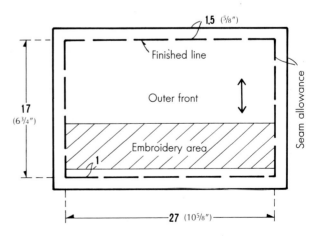

1.5 (5/8″)

Finished line

Outer front

Seam allowance

17 (6¾″)

1

Embroidery area

27 (10⅝″)

See page 27 for embroidery pattern.

Scarfs

Instructions for Dots on page 33 and
for Riceplant on page 34.

Scarfs
Shown on page 32.

MATERIALS: Light Beige scarf for *Dots* design and Drab scarf for *Riceplant*. DMC six-strand embroidery floss, No. 25: For *Dots*: Small amount each of Beige (3021, 3022). Silver lamé thread; For *Riceplant*: Dull Mauve (316), Beige (3022) and Green (3052).

DIRECTIONS: Transfer design onto scarfs and embroider.

Dots

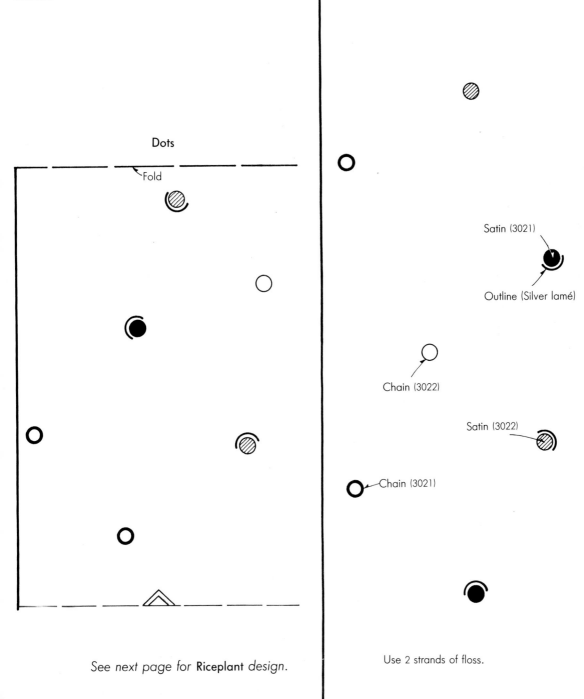

See next page for **Riceplant** design.

Use 2 strands of floss.

Satin (3021)

Outline (Silver lamé)

Chain (3022)

Satin (3022)

Chain (3021)

Fold

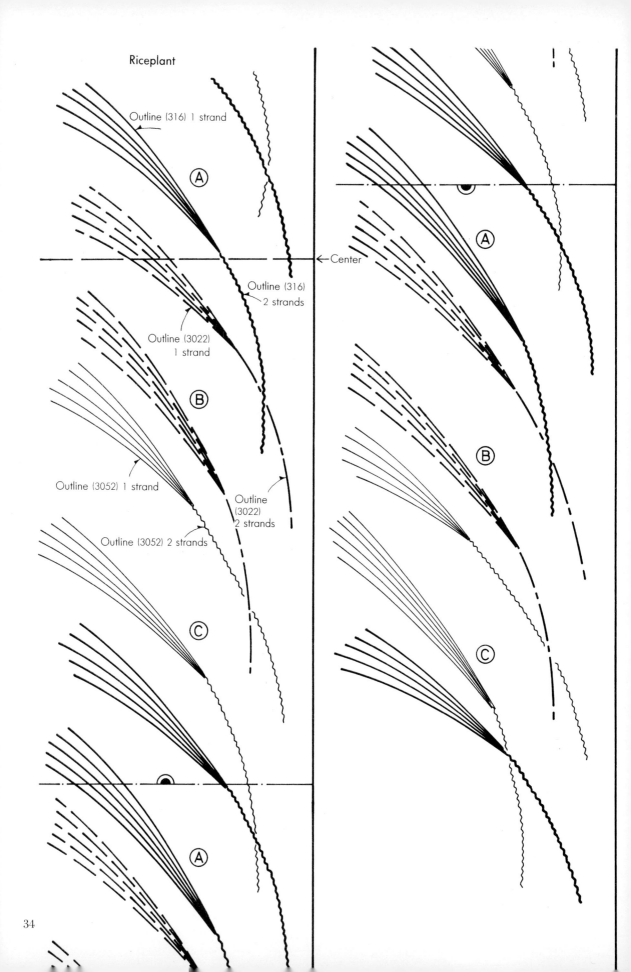

Riceplant

Outline (316) 1 strand

Ⓐ

← Center

Outline (316)
2 strands

Outline (3022)
1 strand

Ⓑ

Outline (3052) 1 strand

Outline
(3022)
2 strands

Outline (3052) 2 strands

Ⓒ

Ⓐ

Ⓑ

Ⓒ

Ⓐ

Heart Picture

Shown on reverse side of cover.

MATERIALS: White linen, 30 cm (11³/₄″) square. DMC six-strand embroidery floss, No. 25: Half skein each of Episcopal Purple (915) and Violet Mauve (340); small amount each of Parma Violet (208), Violet Mauve (340) and Plum (553). Round seed beads (1.7 mm or ¹/₁₆″): 240 Purple, 45 Milky White and 17 Platinum. Frame (see illustration for size).
FINISHED SIZE: Embroidery area: 12 cm by 12 cm (4³/₄″ × 4³/₄″) square.
DIRECTIONS: Transfer design onto linen and embroider. Mount and frame. Sew each bead on French knot with three strands of floss.

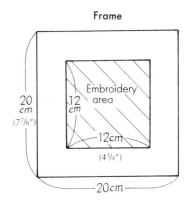

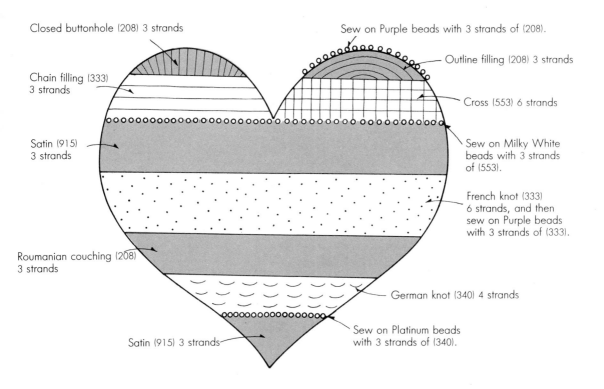

Large Pochette

Shown on page 25.

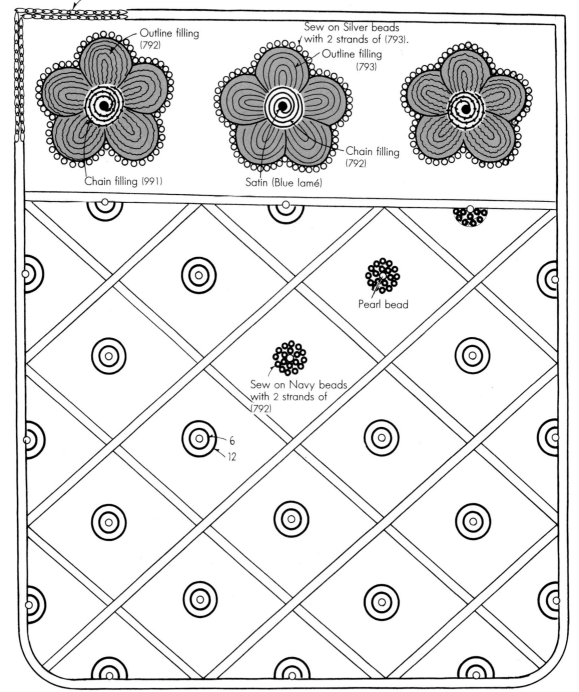

2 rows of chain with Silver lamé.

Outline filling (792)

Sew on Silver beads with 2 strands of (793).

Outline filling (793)

Chain filling (792)

Chain filling (991)

Satin (Blue lamé)

Pearl bead

Sew on Navy beads with 2 strands of (792)

6
12

Use 3 strands of floss unless otherwise directed.

Use lower part of pattern for back.

MATERIALS: Navy linen, 50 cm by 30 cm (19⁵/₈″ × 11³/₄″). Blue Green cotton fabric for lining, 40 cm by 22 cm (15³/₄″ × 8⁵/₈″). DMC six-strand embroidery floss, No. 25: Small amount each of Cornflower Blue (792, 793) and Peacock Green (991). One skein of Silver lamé thread. Small amount of Blue lamé thread. Round seed beads (1.7 mm or ¹/₁₆″): 823 Navy and 180 Platinum. 55 pearl beads, 0.2 cm (¹/₁₆″) in diameter. Iron-on interfacing, 35 cm by 20 cm (13³/₄″ × 7³/₄″). Silver Gray cord, 0.7 cm (¹/₄″) in diameter and 140 cm (55¹/₈″) long. Heart-shaped bead, 1 cm (³/₈″) wide.

FINISHED SIZE: 15 cm wide and 18 cm deep (5⁷/₈″ × 7¹/₈″).

DIRECTIONS: Cut out fabric. Transfer design onto front and back pieces of linen and embroider. Press iron-on interfacing on wrong side of front, gusset, back and strap holder. Sew strap holders. Sew front, gusset and back together catching strap holders. Sew inner pieces together. Insert inner bag into outer one, turn in seam allowance of top edge and slip-stich. Attach crocheted chain loop onto back piece.

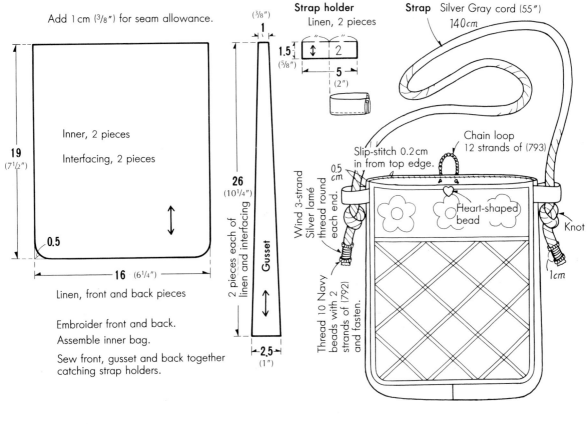

Sash
Shown on page 29.

MATERIALS: Black cotton satin, 30 cm by 150 cm (11³/₄″ × 59″). DMC six-strand embroidery floss, No. 25: One skein of Black (310), Yellow Green (731), Myrtle Gray (927), Antique Blue (931), Sage Green (3012), Green (3051, 3052) and Beige (3022). Silver lamé thread. Round seed beads (1.7 mm or ¹/₁₆″): 2730 frosted Black, 950 glossy Black, 700 Darkish Gold, 400 Blue Gray, 320 Yel-

low Ocher, 250 Khaki, 100 Gray and 14 Silver.

FINISHED SIZE: See diagram.

DIRECTIONS: Cut out front and back pieces. Transfer design onto front and embroider with beads. Turn back seam allowance from fold line, place back piece on wrong side of front and slip-stitch.

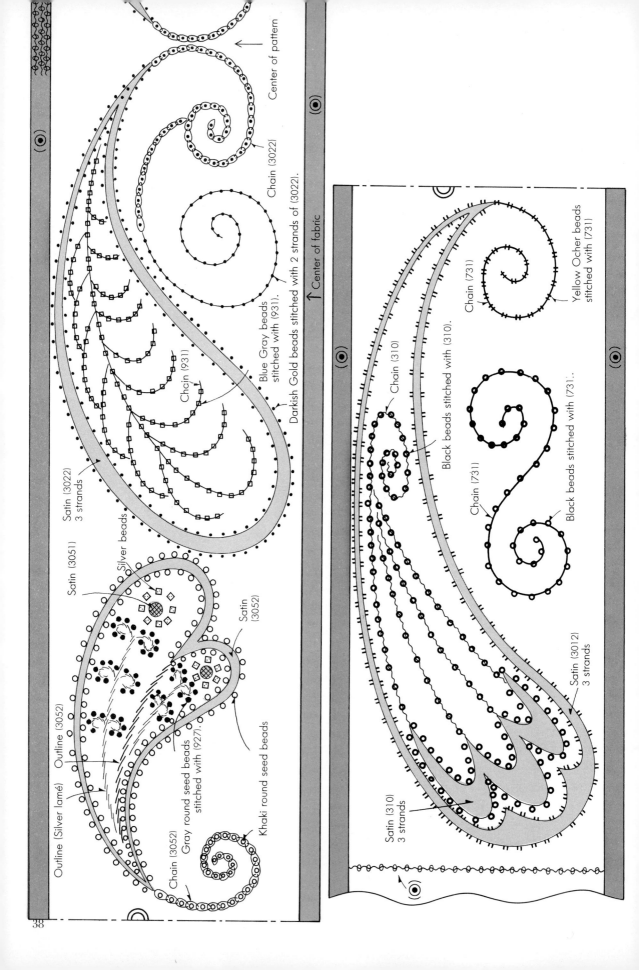

Center of pattern

Chain (3022)

Blue Gray beads
stitched with (931).

Darkish Gold beads stitched with 2 strands of (3022).

↑ Center of fabric

Satin (3022)
3 strands

Chain (931)

Silver beads

Satin (3051)

Satin
(3052)

Outline (Silver lamé)   Outline (3052)

Gray round seed beads
stitched with (927)..

Chain (3052)

Khaki round seed beads

Yellow Ocher beads
stitched with (731)

Chain (731)

Black beads stitched with (310).

Chain (310)

Chain (731)

Black beads stitched with (731)..

Satin (3012)
3 strands

Satin (310)
3 strands

38

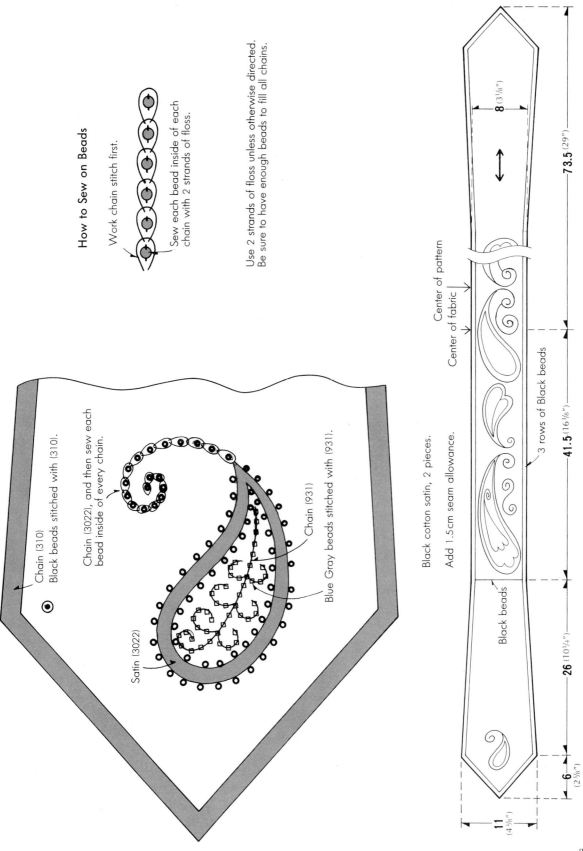

How to Sew on Beads

Work chain stitch first.

Sew each bead inside of each chain with 2 strands of floss.

Use 2 strands of floss unless otherwise directed. Be sure to have enough beads to fill all chains.

Chain (310)
Black beads stitched with (310).

⊙

Chain (3022), and then sew each bead inside of every chain.

Satin (3022)

Chain (931)

Blue Gray beads stitched with (931).

Black cotton satin, 2 pieces.

Add 1.5cm seam allowance.

Center of pattern

Center of fabric

3 rows of Black beads

Black beads

8 (3⅛")

73.5 (29")

41.5 (16⅜")

26 (10¼")

6 (2⅜")

11 (4⅛")

Picture (design)

Shown on page 41.

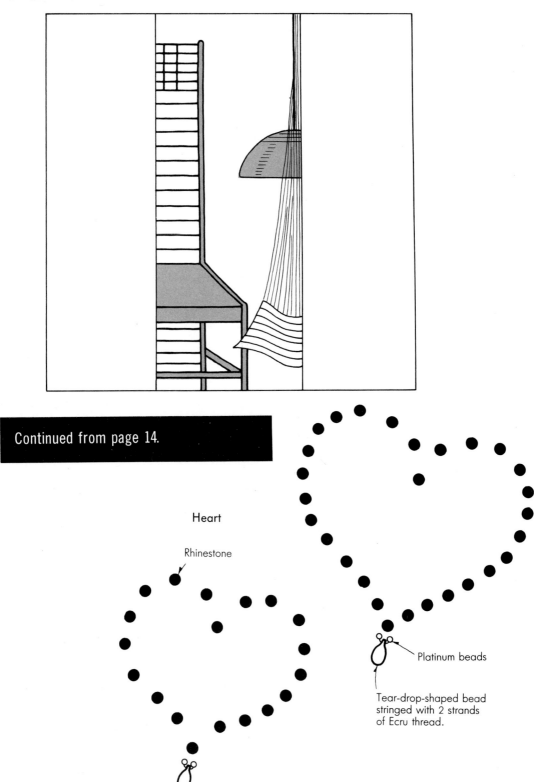

Continued from page 14.

Heart

Rhinestone

Platinum beads

Tear-drop-shaped bead
stringed with 2 strands
of Ecru thread.

P A R T
[2]
INTERIOR

Picture

Design on page 40.

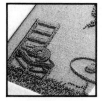

Mini Pictures

Shown on pages 44 & 45.

MATERIALS: Linen: Light Gray for *A*, Blue Gray for *B*, Gray for *C* and Unbleached for *D*, one 25 cm by 20 cm (9⁷/₈″ × 7⁷/₈″) piece each. DMC six-strand embroidery floss, No. 25: Small amount each of Olive Green (520), Almond Green (522, 523) and Myrtle Gray (926) for *A*; Ash Gray (317, 415), Mauve (333), Almond Green (502, 523), Drab (610), Antiqe Blue (932), Moss Green (937, 3364), Dark Brown (3031) and White for *B*; Beaver Gray (648) and White for *C*; Black (310) and Ash Gray (414) for *D*. Silver lamé thread for *A, B, C,* and *D*. Round seed beads (1.7 mm or ¹/₁₆″): One Silver for *B*, Silver Gray for *C* and 6 Pearl Gray for *D*. Frame (see diagram for size).
FINISHED SIZE: See diagram.
DIRECTIONS: Transfer design onto fabric and embroider. Mount and frame.

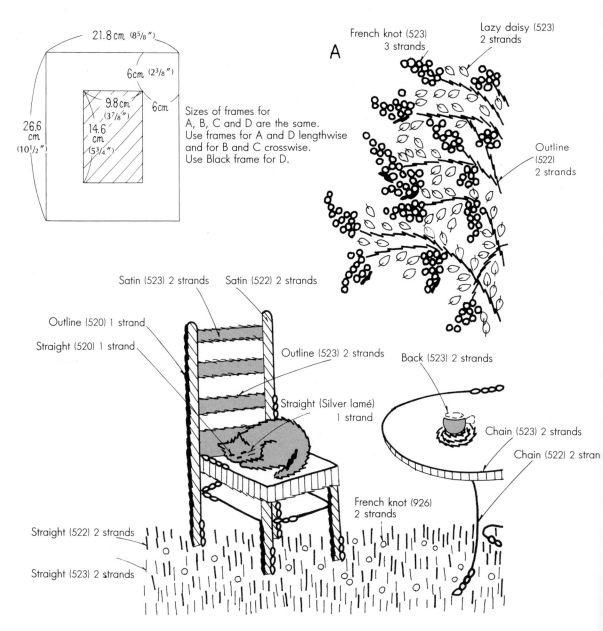

Sizes of frames for
A, B, C and D are the same.
Use frames for A and D lengthwise
and for B and C crosswise.
Use Black frame for D.

21.8 cm (8⁵/₈″)

6 cm (2³/₈″)

9.8 cm (3⁷/₈″)

6 cm

26.6 cm (10¹/₂″)

14.6 cm (5³/₄″)

French knot (523) 3 strands

Lazy daisy (523) 2 strands

A

Outline (522) 2 strands

Satin (523) 2 strands Satin (522) 2 strands

Outline (520) 1 strand

Straight (520) 1 strand

Outline (523) 2 strands

Back (523) 2 strands

Straight (Silver lamé) 1 strand

Chain (523) 2 strands

Chain (522) 2 stran

French knot (926) 2 strands

Straight (522) 2 strands

Straight (523) 2 strands

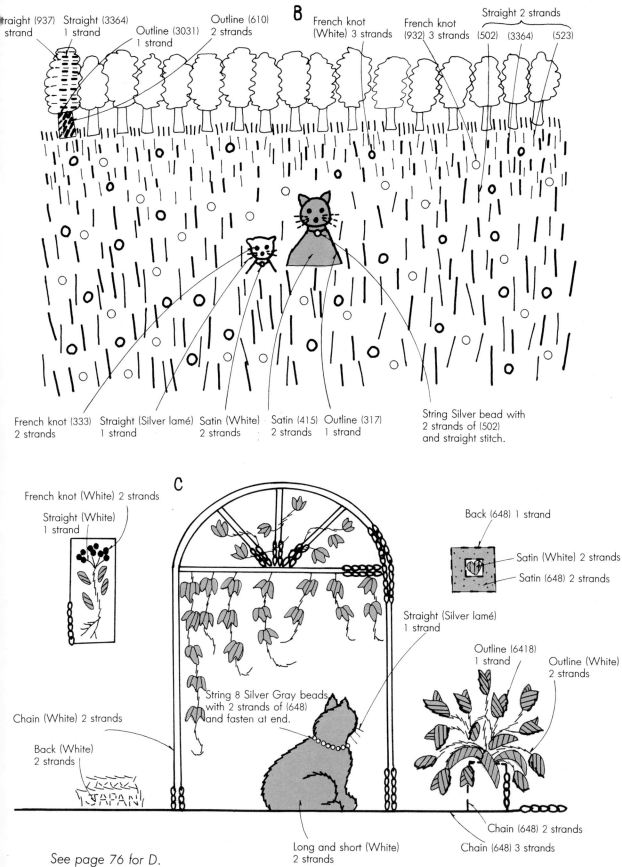

B

Straight (937) 1 strand

Straight (3364) 1 strand

Outline (3031) 1 strand

Outline (610) 2 strands

French knot (White) 3 strands

French knot (932) 3 strands

Straight 2 strands
(502)　(3364)　(523)

French knot (333) 2 strands

Straight (Silver lamé) 1 strand

Satin (White) 2 strands

Satin (415) 2 strands

Outline (317) 1 strand

String Silver bead with 2 strands of (502) and straight stitch.

C

French knot (White) 2 strands

Straight (White) 1 strand

Back (648) 1 strand

Satin (White) 2 strands

Satin (648) 2 strands

Straight (Silver lamé) 1 strand

Outline (6418) 1 strand

Outline (White) 2 strands

Chain (White) 2 strands

Back (White) 2 strands

String 8 Silver Gray beads with 2 strands of (648) and fasten at end.

Chain (648) 2 strands

Chain (648) 3 strands

Long and short (White) 2 strands

See page 76 for D.

43

Mini Pictures

Instructions for A on page 42, for B and C on
page 43 and for D on page 76.

C

D

Cat-shaped Pillows
Shown on pages 48 & 49.

MATERIALS: Light Beige linen with black dots and Beige linen, 85 cm by 30 cm (33$\frac{1}{2}$″ × 11$\frac{3}{4}$″) each. White cotton polyester fabric for inner pillow, 85 cm by 30 cm (33$\frac{1}{2}$″ × 11$\frac{3}{4}$″). DMC six-strand embroidery floss, No. 25: Small amount each of Black (310), Black mohair yarn (same thickness as baby yarn), Gold and Silver lamé

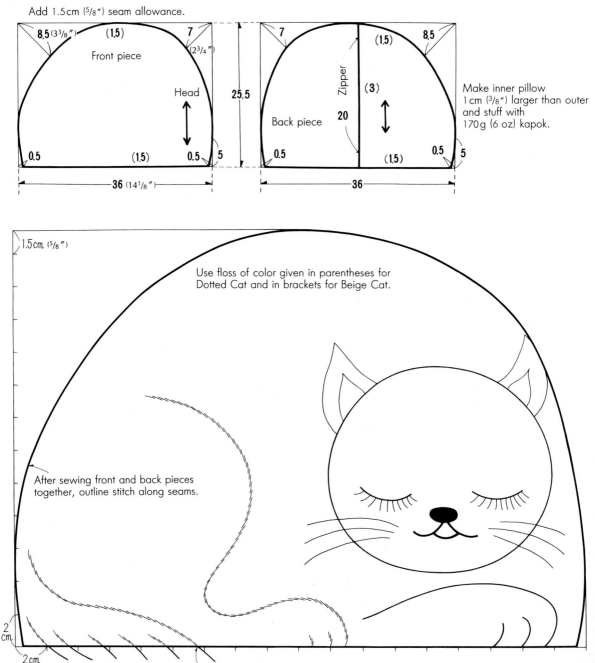

Add 1.5 cm ($\frac{5}{8}$″) seam allowance.

8.5 (3$\frac{3}{8}$″) (1,5) 7

Front piece

(2$\frac{3}{4}$″)

Head

25.5

0.5 (1,5) 0.5 5

36 (14$\frac{1}{8}$″)

7 (1,5) 8.5

Zipper

(3)

Back piece 20

0.5 (1,5) 0.5 5

36

Make inner pillow 1 cm ($\frac{3}{8}$″) larger than outer and stuff with 170 g (6 oz) kapok.

1.5 cm ($\frac{5}{8}$″)

Use floss of color given in parentheses for Dotted Cat and in brackets for Beige Cat.

After sewing front and back pieces together, outline stitch along seams.

2 cm

2 cm

Leave 4–5 cm (2″) yarn, start with one backstitch and continue to outline stitch.

threads. Silver bell, 0.8cm ($^3/_8$″) in diameter. 20cm ($7^7/_8$″) long zipper. Kapok, 170g (6 oz) for each.
FINISHED SIZE: See diagram.
DIRECTIONS: Reverse pattern for second pillow. Transfer design onto fabric and embroider. Sew zipper onto back pieces. Sew front and back together. Outline stitch along edge and outline of legs and paws. Attach bell in place. Make inner pillow 1 cm ($^3/_8$″) larger than outer one and insert into embroidered pillow.

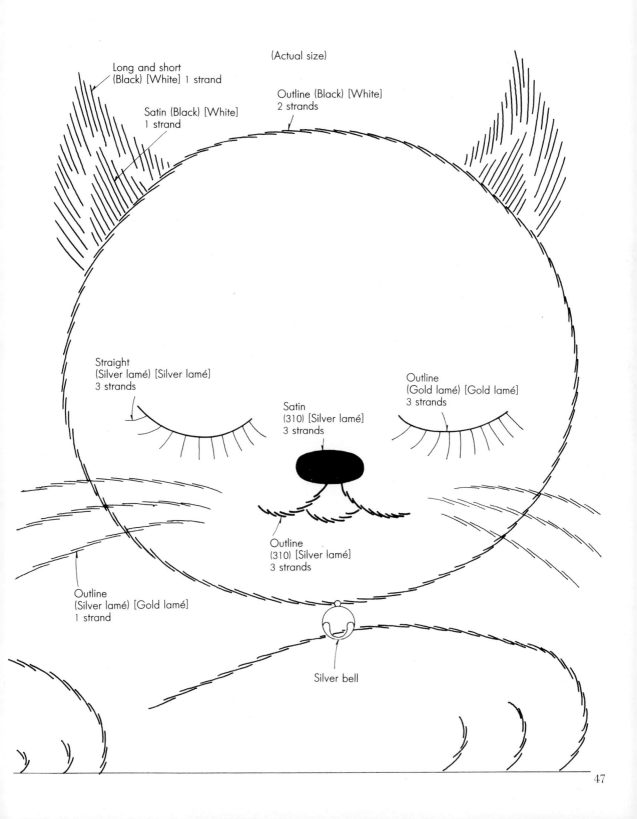

(Actual size)

Long and short
(Black) [White] 1 strand

Outline (Black) [White]
2 strands

Satin (Black) [White]
1 strand

Straight
(Silver lamé) [Silver lamé]
3 strands

Satin
(310) [Silver lamé]
3 strands

Outline
(Gold lamé) [Gold lamé]
3 strands

Outline
(310) [Silver lamé]
3 strands

Outline
(Silver lamé) [Gold lamé]
1 strand

Silver bell

Cat-shaped Pillows
Instructions on page 46.

48

Rectangular Pillow

Shown on pages 52 & 53.

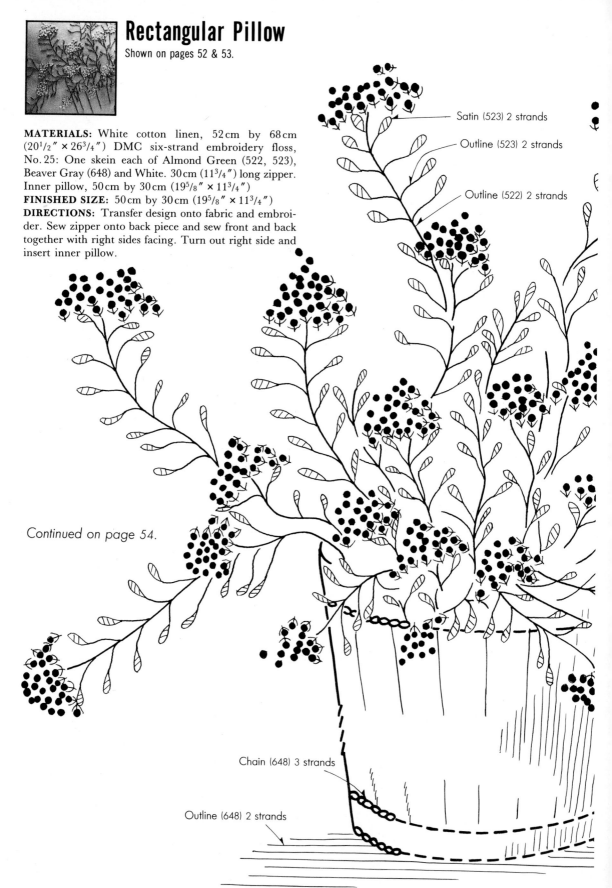

MATERIALS: White cotton linen, 52 cm by 68 cm (20 1/2″ × 26 3/4″) DMC six-strand embroidery floss, No. 25: One skein each of Almond Green (522, 523), Beaver Gray (648) and White. 30 cm (11 3/4″) long zipper. Inner pillow, 50 cm by 30 cm (19 5/8″ × 11 3/4″).

FINISHED SIZE: 50 cm by 30 cm (19 5/8″ × 11 3/4″)

DIRECTIONS: Transfer design onto fabric and embroider. Sew zipper onto back piece and sew front and back together with right sides facing. Turn out right side and insert inner pillow.

Continued on page 54.

Satin (523) 2 strands

Outline (523) 2 strands

Outline (522) 2 strands

Chain (648) 3 strands

Outline (648) 2 strands

French knot (White) 3 strands

Fly (523) 2 strands

Outline (648) 3 strands
Outline (648) 2 strands

51

Rectangular Pillow

Instructions on page 50.

Continued from page 50.

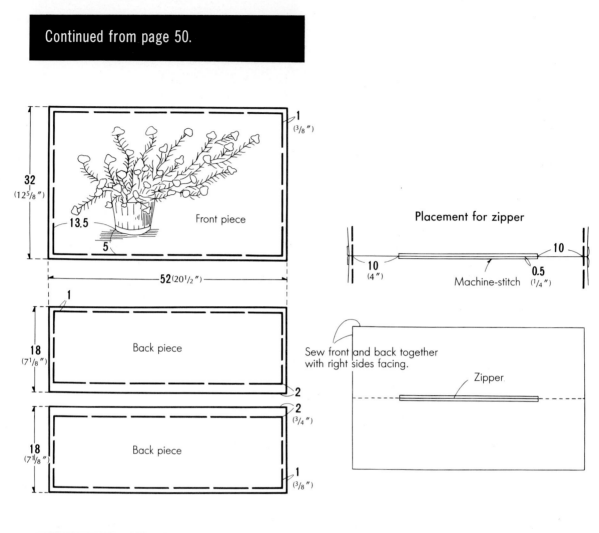

Placement for zipper

32 (12⁵/₈″)

13.5

5

Front piece

52 (20¹/₂″)

1 (³/₈″)

10 (4″)

10

0.5 (¹/₄″)

Machine-stitch

18 (7¹/₈″)

Back piece

1

2

Sew front and back together with right sides facing.

Zipper

18 (7¹/₈″)

Back piece

2

2 (³/₄″)

1 (³/₈″)

Kitchen Picture

Shown on page 57.

MATERIALS: Blue linen, 30cm by 25cm (11³/₄″ × 9⁷/₈″). DMC six-strand embroidery floss, No. 25: One skein each of Cornflower Blue (793) and Drab (611); small amount each of Green (3051, 3052, 3053), Dark Brown (3031, 3033), Beige (3022), Sage Green (3012), Cornflower Blue (791), Yellow Green (731), Smoke Gray (642) and Ecru. Silver and Gold lamé threads. Round seed beads (1.7 mm or ¹/₁₆″): 5 Yellow Ocher, 4 Dark Red and 2 Khaki. Frame (see diagram for size).
FINISHED SIZE: See diagram.
DIRECTIONS: Transfer design onto fabric and embroider. Mount and frame.

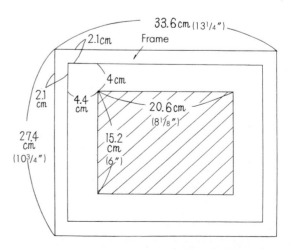

33.6 cm (13¹/₄″)

Frame

2.1 cm

2.1 cm

4 cm

4.4 cm

20.6 cm (8¹/₈″)

27.4 cm (10³/₄″)

15.2 cm (6″)

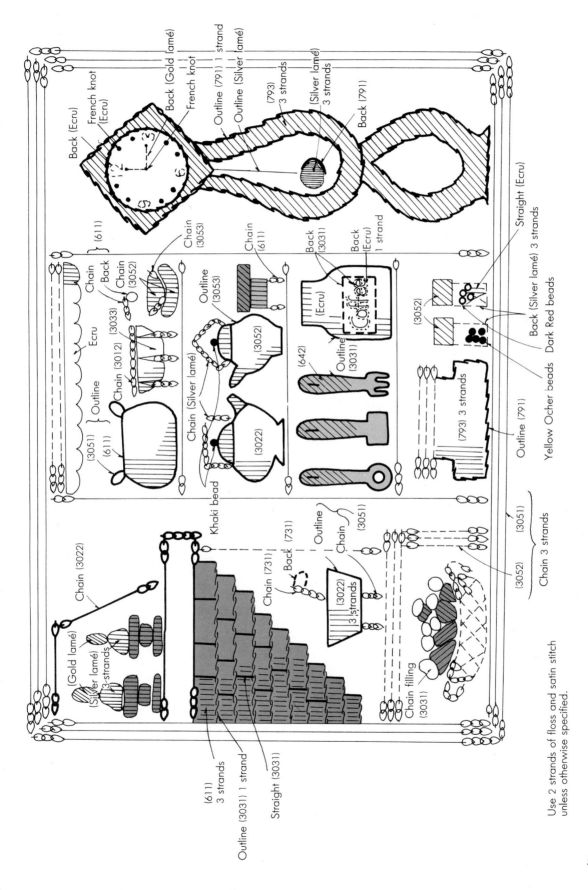

Back (Ecru)
French knot (Ecru)
Back (Gold lamé)
French knot
Outline (791) 1 strand
Outline (Silver lamé)
(793) 3 strands
(Silver lamé) 3 strands
Back (791)
Straight (Ecru)

(611)
Chain (3053)
Chain (611)
Back (3031)
Back (Ecru) 1 strand
Back (Silver lamé) 3 strands
Dark Red beads

Chain
Chain
Back
Chain (3052)
Outline (3053)
(3052)
(642)
Outline (3031)
(3052)

Chain (3033)
Ecru
Chain (3012)
Chain (Silver lamé)
(3022)
(793) 3 strands
Outline (791)
Yellow Ocher beads

Outline (3051) (611)
Khaki bead

Chain (3022)
(Gold lamé)
(Silver lamé) 3-strands
Back (731)
Outline Chain (3051)
(731)
(3022) 3 strands
Chain 3 strands
(3052)
(3051)

(611) 3 strands
Outline (3031) 1 strand
Straight (3031)
Chain filling (3031)

Use 2 strands of floss and satin stitch unless otherwise specified.

55

Kitchen Pictures

Instructions for Picture at left on page 58 and
for Picture at right on page 54.

Kitchen Picture

Shown on page 56.

MATERIALS: Blue Gray Indian cloth (51 threads by 49.5 threads per 10 cm square), 40 cm by 30 cm (15³/₄″ × 11³/₄″). DMC six-strand embroidery floss, No. 25: 2¹/₂ skeins of Smoke Gray (642); one skein each of Drab (610, 611, 612), Smoke Gray (644), Beige (3022), Green (3051, 3052, 3053, 3362, 3363), Moss Green (469), Antique Blue

One square represents one square of fabric.

Use 3 strands of floss unless otherwise directed.

(930, 931, 932), Ash Gray (415) and Ecru; small amount each of Smoke Gray (822), Almond Green (502), Yellow Green (732) and Moss Green (937). Silver lamé thread. 6 wooden beads, 0.5 cm (¼″) in diameter. Frame (see diagram for size).

FINISHED SIZE: See diagram.

DIRECTIONS: Work cross-stitch and other stitches following chart below. Mount and frame.

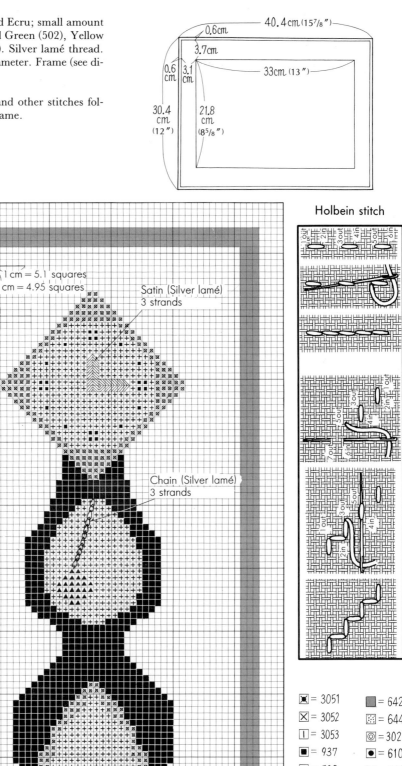

Chain
(3022)

1 cm = 5.1 squares
1 cm = 4.95 squares

Satin (Silver lamé)
3 strands

Chain
(3052)

Chain (Silver lamé)
3 strands

Chain
(610)

Satin
(3053)

Holbein stitch

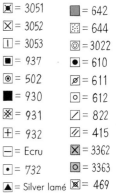

⊠ = 3051		▦ = 642
✕ = 3052		▦ = 644
▯ = 3053		◎ = 3022
■ = 937		● = 610
⊙ = 502		⊘ = 611
■ = 930		▢ = 612
⊠ = 931		╱ = 822
✚ = 932		⊘ = 415
⊟ = Ecru		⊠ = 3362
▪ = 732		◎ = 3363
▲ = Silver lamé		⊠ = 469

59

Rooster Potholders

Instructions on page 62.

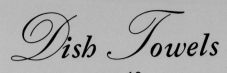

Dish Towels

Instructions on page 62.

Dish Towels

Shown on page 61.

MATERIALS: Materials for Red-checked towel are indicated in brackets. Blue-checked cotton [Red-checked], 80 cm by 50 cm ($31^{1}/_{2}$" × $19^{5}/_{8}$"). DMC six-strand embroidery floss, No. 25: Half skein each of Cornflower Blue (791) [Green (3052)] and Green (561) [Scarlet (304)]. Green [Red] bias tape, 2 cm by 270 cm ($^{3}/_{4}$" × 9'). **FINISHED SIZE:** 50 cm by 80 cm ($19^{5}/_{8}$" × $31^{1}/_{2}$"). **DIRECTIONS:** Bind edges with bias tape. Transfer design onto towel and embroider. Use 3 strands of floss unless otherwise directed.

Directions are given for Blue-checked towel, with changes for Red-checked towel noted in brackets.

Use 3 strands of floss unless otherwise directed.

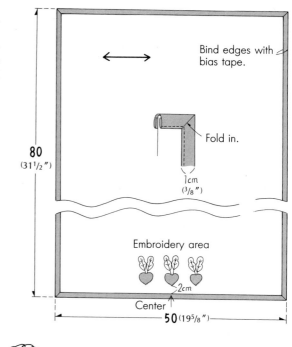

Bind edges with bias tape.

Fold in.

1 cm ($^{3}/_{8}$")

80 ($31^{1}/_{2}$")

Embroidery area

2 cm

Center

50 ($19^{5}/_{8}$")

Chain (791) [3052]

Outline (791) [3052]

Outline (561) [304] 2 strands

Roumanian couching (561) [304]

Center

Rooster Potholders

Shown on page 60.

MATERIALS: Materials for Potholder with Brown crest are indicated in brackets. Moss Green quilted fabric, 90 cm by 20 cm ($35^{3}/_{8}$" × $7^{7}/_{8}$"). Scrap of Blue Green [Dark Brown] fabric. DMC six-strand embroidery floss, No. 25: Small amount each of Olive Green (520) [Dark Brown (3031) and Antique Blue (931) [Olive Green (522)].

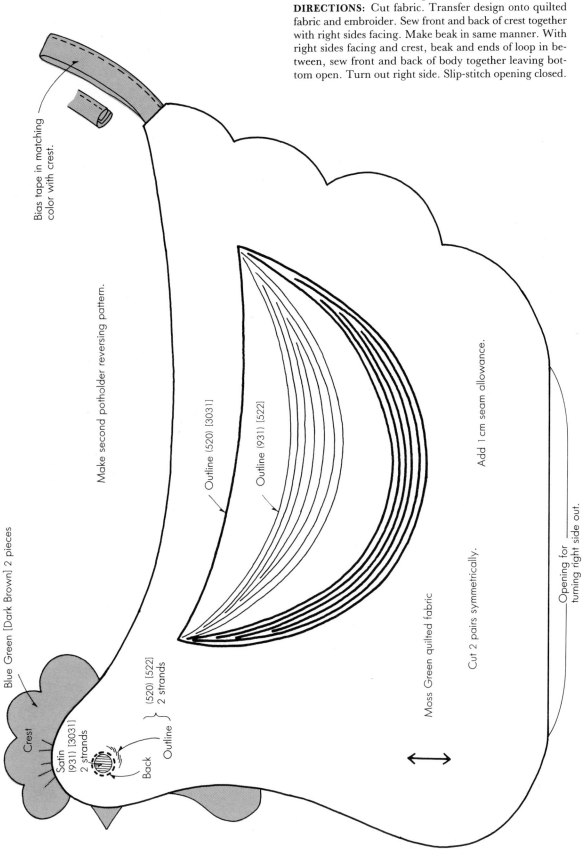

FINISHED SIZE: See diagram.

DIRECTIONS: Cut fabric. Transfer design onto quilted fabric and embroider. Sew front and back of crest together with right sides facing. Make beak in same manner. With right sides facing and crest, beak and ends of loop in between, sew front and back of body together leaving bottom open. Turn out right side. Slip-stitch opening closed.

Bias tape in matching color with crest.

Make second potholder reversing pattern.

Outline (520) [3031]

Outline (931) [522]

Add 1 cm seam allowance.

Moss Green quilted fabric

Cut 2 pairs symmetrically.

Opening for turning right side out.

Blue Green [Dark Brown] 2 pieces

Crest

Satin (931) [3031] 2 strands

(520) [522] 2 strands

Back

Outline

Pictures—Table and Cottage

Instructions for Table Picture on page 74 and
for Cottage Picture on page 66.

Cottage Picture

Shown on page 65.

Use 2 strands of floss unless otherwise directed.

Unbleached woolen yarn

Outline filling 3 strands

(580)

(581)

(3051) { Outline
          Satin

Satin

(Ecru)   (535)

(518)   Satin (640)
               (3051)

(648)

Outline
(535)

Long and short
(517) 3 strands

Chain (Ecru)   Straight (646)

Balcony

Outline (518)

French knot
(3021)
3 strands

Long and short
(580)

(731)

(581)

Satin (White)

French knot (793) 3 strands

French knot (518)

MATERIALS: Moss Green linen, 32 cm by 28 cm (12⅝″ × 11″). DMC six-strand embroidery floss, No. 25: 2 skeins of Beaver Gray (648); 1 skein each of Golden Green (580, 581); ½ skein of Sky Blue (517); small amount each of Sky Blue (518), Antique Gray (535), Ash Gray (317, 414), Beaver Gray (646, 647), Yellow Green (731, 734), Copper Green (830, 832), Beige (3021), Ivy Green (501), Green (3051), Myrtle Gray (926), Smoke Gray (640), Saffron (725), Raspberry Red (3608), Cornflower Blue (793), Ecru and White. Unbleached and Light Blue woolen yarn. Frame (see diagram for size).

FINISHED SIZE: See diagram.

DIRECTIONS: Transfer design onto fabric and embroider. Brush woolen yarn to puff up and glue in place. Mount and frame.

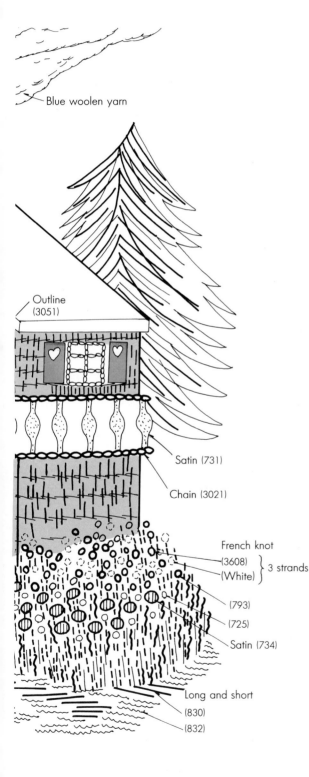

Blue woolen yarn

Outline (3051)

Satin (731)

Chain (3021)

French knot
(3608)
(White) } 3 strands

(793)

(725)

Satin (734)

Long and short
(830)
(832)

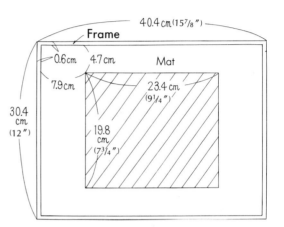

Frame

40.4 cm (15⅞″)

0.6 cm   4.7 cm   Mat

7.9 cm   23.4 cm (9¼″)

30.4 cm (12″)

19.8 cm (7¾″)

Door
Outline alternating (580) and (3051).

Balcony (Arrange properly.)

Lazy daisy (580)
Outline (581)
French knot (725) 3 strands

Bay window (Arrange properly.)

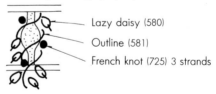

French knot (725)
Lazy daisy (580)
Outline (580)

Stone wall
Long and short
A = (647) (414)
B = (501) (317)
C = (926) (317)
Outline edge with (535)

Table Runner

Instructions on page 70.

Table Runner

Shown on pages 68 & 69.

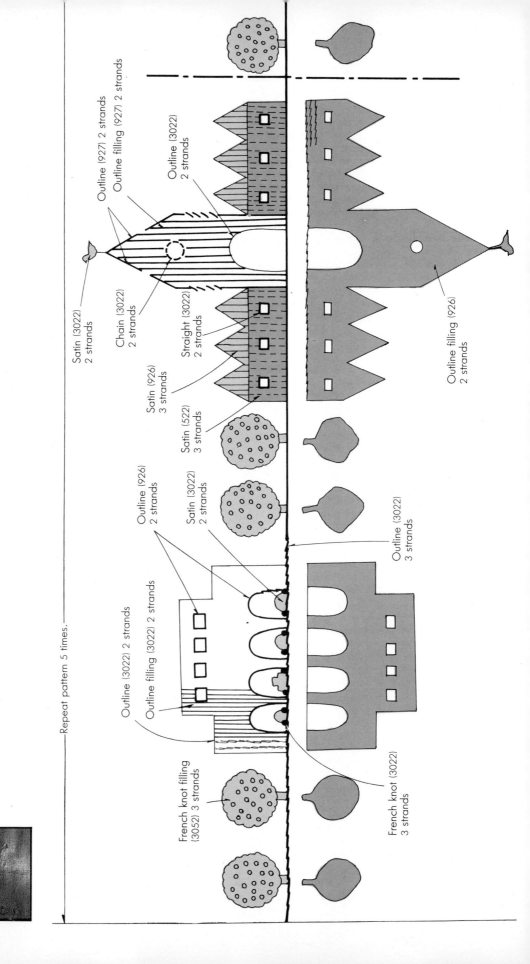

Repeat pattern 5 times.

Outline (927) 2 strands
Outline filling (927) 2 strands

Outline (3022) 2 strands

Satin (3022) 2 strands

Chain (3022) 2 strands

Straight (3022) 2 strands

Satin (926) 3 strands

Satin (522) 3 strands

Outline filling (926) 2 strands

Outline (926) 2 strands

Satin (3022) 2 strands

Outline (3022) 2 strands

Outline filling (3022) 2 strands

Outline (3022) 3 strands

French knot filling (3052) 3 strands

French knot (3022) 3 strands

70

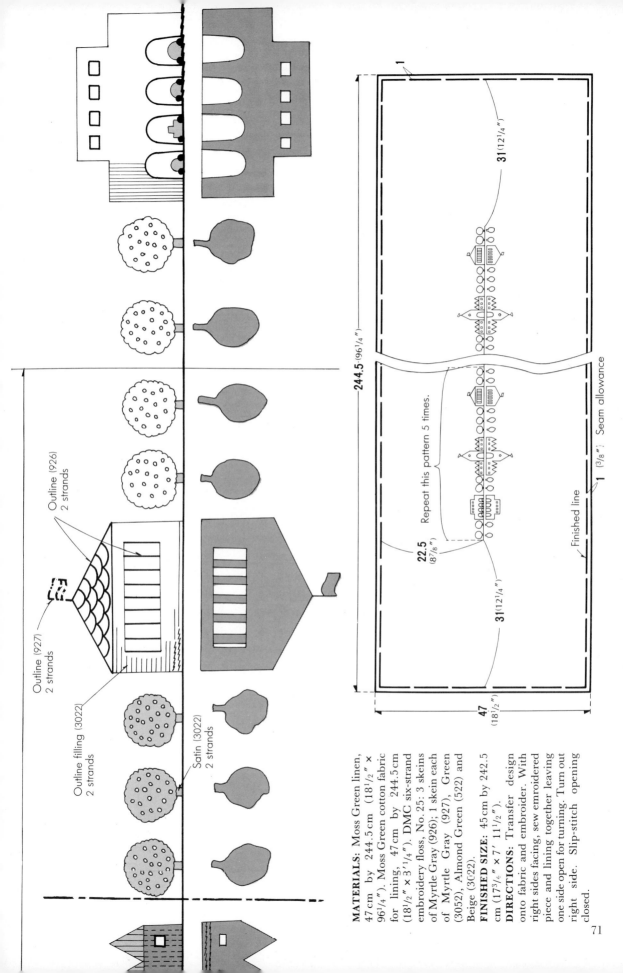

Outline (926)
2 strands

Outline (927)
2 strands

Outline filling (3022)
2 strands

Satin (3022)
2 strands

1

31 (12¹/₄")

244.5 (96¹/₄")

Repeat this pattern 5 times.

22.5 (8⁷/₈")

31 (12¹/₄")

Finished line

1 (³/₈") Seam allowance

47 (18¹/₂")

MATERIALS: Moss Green linen, 47 cm by 244.5 cm (18¹/₂" × 96¹/₄"). Moss Green cotton fabric for lining, 47 cm by 244.5 cm (18¹/₂" × 3'1¹/₄"). DMC six-strand embroidery floss, No. 25: 3 skeins of Myrtle Gray (926); 1 skein each of Myrtle Gray (927), Green (3052), Almond Green (522) and Beige (3022).

FINISHED SIZE: 45 cm by 242.5 cm (17³/₄" × 7' 11¹/₂").

DIRECTIONS: Transfer design onto fabric and embroider. With right sides facing, sew emroidered piece and lining together leaving one side open for turning. Turn out right side. Slip-stitch opening closed.

71

Mini Mats

Instructions on page 73.

Mini Mats

Shown on page 72.

MATERIALS: Blue Gray Indian cloth (5 threads per 1 cm), 9.5 cm (3³/₄″) square for *Ocean* and Blue Gray cotton fabric, 9.5 cm square for *Sea Gull*. For *Ocean*: DMC six-strand embroidery floss, No. 25: Small amount each of Antique Blue (930, 931), Almond Green (502), Ecru, Mauve (333) and Green (3051). Silver and Gold lamé threads. Unbleached woolen yarn. For *Sea Gull*: DMC six-strand embroidery floss, No. 25: Small amount each of Mauve (340), Almond Green (503), Yellow Green (731), Antique Blue (931, 932), Beige (3022) and Ecru. Silver lamé thread. Unbleached woolen yarn. Acrylic clear box (see diagram for size).

FINISHED SIZE: See diagram.

DIRECTIONS: Work cross-stitch following chart. Draw out fabric threads to make fringe.

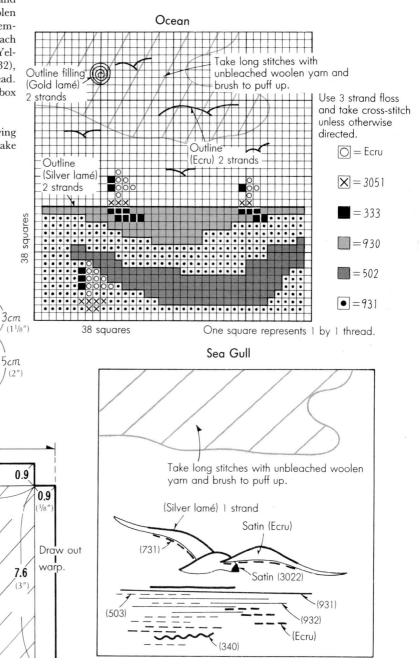

Ocean

Outline filling (Gold lamé) 2 strands

Take long stitches with unbleached woolen yarn and brush to puff up.

Use 3 strand floss and take cross-stitch unless otherwise directed.

Outline (Silver lamé) 2 strands

Outline (Ecru) 2 strands

38 squares

38 squares

One square represents 1 by 1 thread.

- ◻ = Ecru
- ☒ = 3051
- ◼ = 333
- ◻ = 930
- ◼ = 502
- ● = 931

10cm

10cm (3⁷/₈″)

7.6 cm   7.6 cm

3cm (1¹/₈″)

5cm (2″)

9.4 (3³/₄″)

Draw out weft.   0.9

7.6   0.9 (3/8″)

Draw out warp.

9.4

Embroidery area   7.6 (3″)

Sea Gull

Take long stitches with unbleached woolen yarn and brush to puff up.

(Silver lamé) 1 strand

Satin (Ecru)

(731)

Satin (3022)

(503)

(931)

(932)

(Ecru)

(340)

Use 2 strand floss and take outline stitch unless otherwise directed.

Table Picture

Shown on page 64.

MATERIALS: Moss Green linen, 19 cm by 20 cm (7½″ × 7⅞″). DMC six-strand embroidery floss, No. 25: Small amount each of Drab (610), Myrtle Gray (926), Sage Green (3011), Green (3051) and Ecru. Unbleached woolen yarn. 10 Platinum round seed beads (1.7 mm or ¹/₁₆″). Frame (see diagram for size).

FINISHED SIZE: See diagram.

DIRECTIONS: Transfer design onto fabric and embroider. Straight stitches with woolen yarn and brush to puff up. Mount and frame.

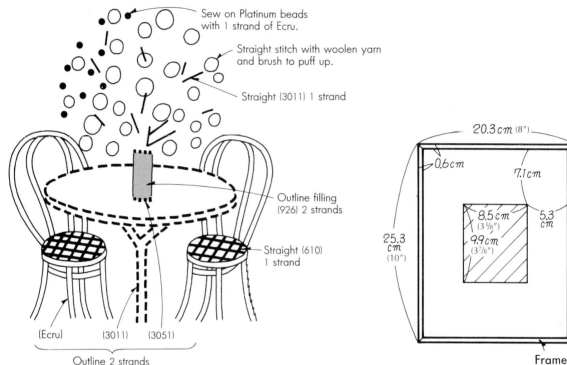

Sew on Platinum beads with 1 strand of Ecru.

Straight stitch with woolen yarn and brush to puff up.

Straight (3011) 1 strand

Outline filling (926) 2 strands

Straight (610) 1 strand

(Ecru) (3011) (3051)

Outline 2 strands

20.3cm (8″)

0.6cm

7.1cm

8.5cm (3⅜″)

9.9cm (3⅞″)

5.3 cm

25.3 cm (10″)

Frame

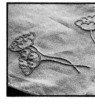

Table Center

Shown on page 101.

MATERIALS: Lightweight White linen, 91 cm (35⅞″) square. DMC six-strand embroidery floss, No. 25: One skein of White. Silver lamé thread.

FINISHED SIZE: 89 cm (35″) square.

DIRECTIONS: Transfer design onto fabric reversing pattern for left side and upper half. Embroider. Fold edges twice and slipstitch.

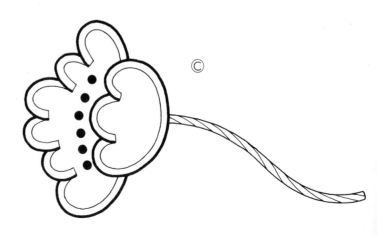

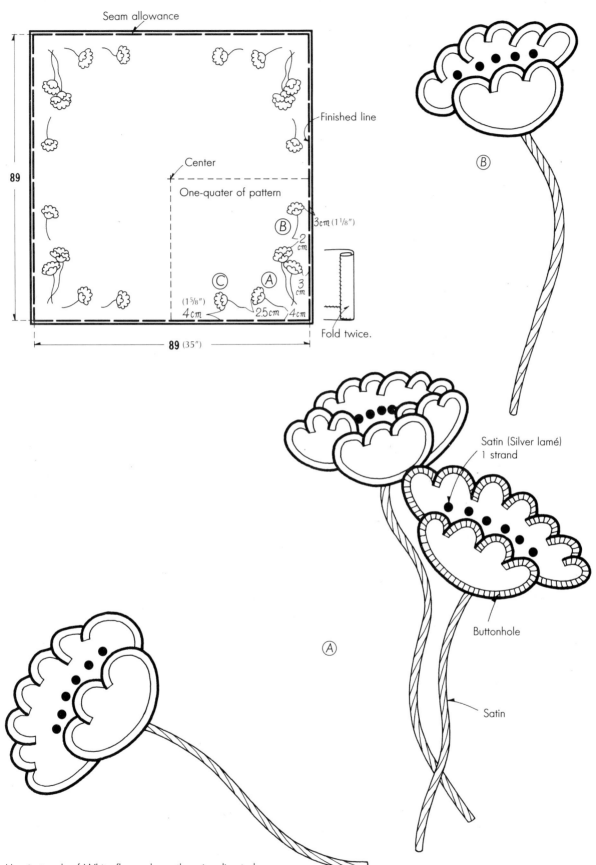

Seam allowance

Finished line

Center

One-quater of pattern

89

B

3cm (1 1/8")

2 cm

C

A

3 cm

(1 5/8")
4cm

2.5cm

4cm

Fold twice.

89 (35")

B

Satin (Silver lamé)
1 strand

Buttonhole

Satin

A

Use 2 strands of White floss unless otherwise directed.

Continued from page 43.

Outline filling
2 strands

Chain 2 strands

French knot
Back   } 1 strand
Chain

Satin
2 strands

String Pearl Gray beads with
1 strand of (414) and
stitch end(s).

Outline (Silver lamé) 1 strand

Outline (414) 1 strand

Long and short 2 strands

Use (310) floss unless otherwise directed.

Outline 1 strand
Outline 2 strands

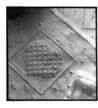

Mats

Shown on page 109.

MATERIALS for two mats: Off-white linen (10.8 threads per 10 cm), 55 cm by 27 cm ($21^5/_8'' \times 10^5/_8''$). DMC six-strand embroidery floss, No. 25: Half skein of Ecru. **FINISHED SIZE:** 23 cm (9″) square.

DIRECTIONS: Mark center of linen and work cross-stitch following chart. Work four-sided stitch along hem line. Fold edges twice and hemstitch mitering corners. Work detached cross stitches referring to photo on page 109.

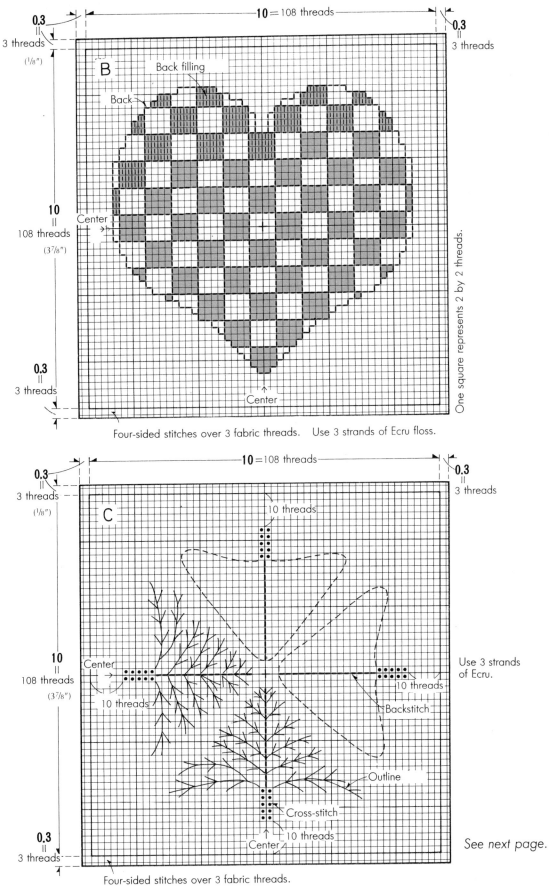

B

Back filling

Back

10 = 108 threads

0.3
‖
3 threads
(1/8″)

0.3
‖
3 threads

10
‖
108 threads
(3⁷/₈″)

Center

One square represents 2 by 2 threads.

Center

Four-sided stitches over 3 fabric threads.   Use 3 strands of Ecru floss.

C

10 = 108 threads

0.3
‖
3 threads

0.3
‖
3 threads
(1/8″)

10 threads

10
‖
108 threads
(3⁷/₈″)

Center

Use 3 strands of Ecru.

10 threads

10 threads

Backstitch

Outline

Cross-stitch

10 threads

Center

See next page.

Four-sided stitches over 3 fabric threads.

0.3
‖
3 threads

77

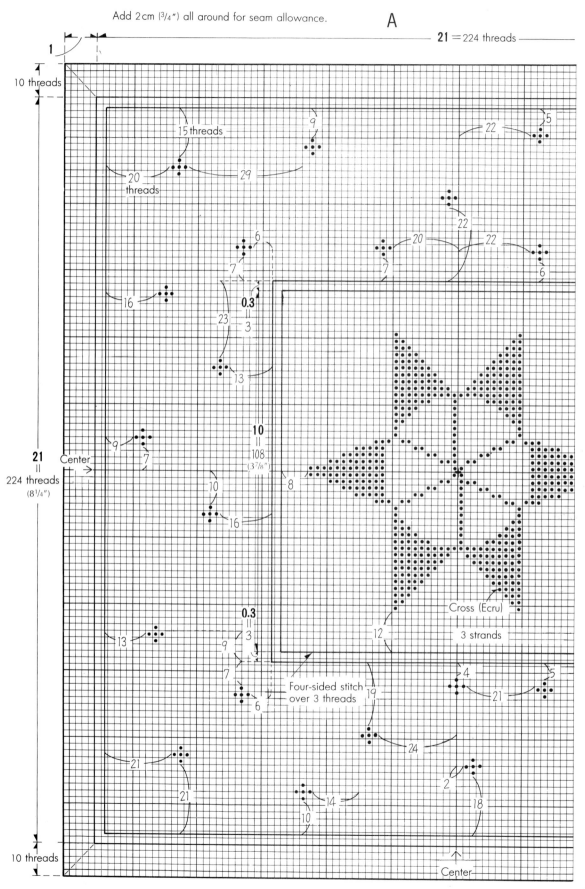

Add 2cm (³/₄") all around for seam allowance.

A

21 = 224 threads

1

10 threads

15 threads

20 threads

29

9

22

5

6

7

20

7

22

22

6

16

23

0.3
3

13

9

7

Center

10

16

10
108
(3⁷/₈")

8

Cross (Ecru)

3 strands

0.3
3

13

9

7

6

12

Four-sided stitch
over 3 threads

19

4

21

5

24

21

21

21

14

10

2

18

10 threads

Center

21
224 threads
(8¼")

78

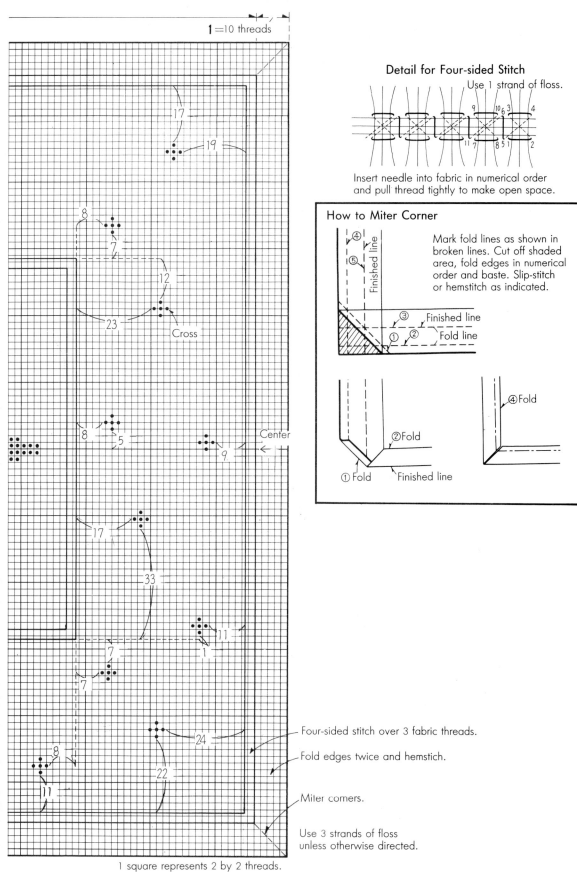

1 = 10 threads

Detail for Four-sided Stitch

Use 1 strand of floss.

Insert needle into fabric in numerical order and pull thread tightly to make open space.

How to Miter Corner

Mark fold lines as shown in broken lines. Cut off shaded area, fold edges in numerical order and baste. Slip-stitch or hemstitch as indicated.

Finished line
Fold line
③ Finished line
① ② Fold line

② Fold
① Fold
Finished line

④ Fold

17
19
8
7
12
23
Cross
8
5
9
Center
17
33
11
7
1
7
24
22
8
11

Four-sided stitch over 3 fabric threads.

Fold edges twice and hemstich.

Miter corners.

Use 3 strands of floss unless otherwise directed.

1 square represents 2 by 2 threads.

Picture (design)
Shown on page 81.

Continued from page 107.

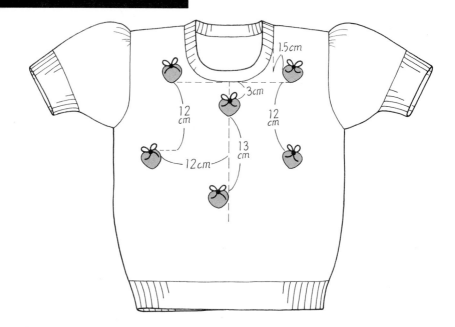

PART

[3]

P A R T

G I F T

Picture

Design on
page 80.

Picture
Shown on page 84.

MATERIALS: Beige cotton satin, 25 cm (9⁷/₈″) square. DMC six-strand embroidery floss, No. 25: Small amount each of Dull Mauve (316), Almond Green (502), Olive Green (520), Drab (611), Myrtle Gray (927), Dark Brown (3031), Green (3052) and Ecru. Silver lamé thread. 22 Pale Claret round seed beads (1.7 mm or ¹/₁₆″). One White round bead, 0.2 cm (¹/₁₆″) in diameter. Frame (see diagram for size).

FINISHED SIZE: See diagram.

DIRECTIONS: Transfer design onto fabric and embroider. Mount and frame.

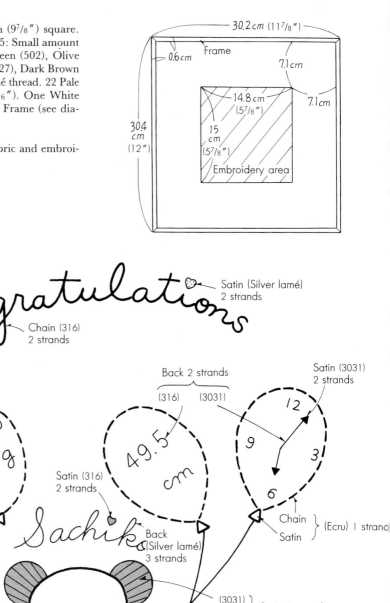

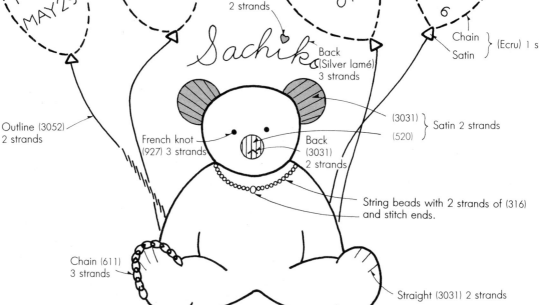

Bell Pull

Shown on page 85.

MATERIALS: Blue Gray linen, 18 cm by 36 cm (7″ × 14¹/₈″). DMC six-strand embroidery floss, No. 25: Small amount each of Ecru, Raspberry Red (3608), Moss Green (3363, 3364), Beige (3023), Parma Violet (208), Antique Blue (931), Ivy Green (501) and Myrtle Gray (926). Silver lamé thread. Raspberry Red semi-transparent and Blue round beads, 0.3 cm (¹/₈″) in diameter, one each. One pair of bell pull attachments, 8 cm (3¹/₈″) wide. Heart-shaped wood, 3 cm (1¹/₈″) long. 2 shell buttons, 1 cm (³/₈″) in diameter.

FINISHED SIZE: 30 cm long and 7 cm wide (11³/₄″ × 2³/₄″).

DIRECTIONS: Transfer design onto fabric and embroider. Sew on beads and buttons. Fold each side to back, turn in seam allowance of one side and slip-stitch. Turn over top and bottom hems through attachments and slip-stitch. Attach heart-shaped wood with bead.

Use 3 strands of floss
unless otherwise directed.

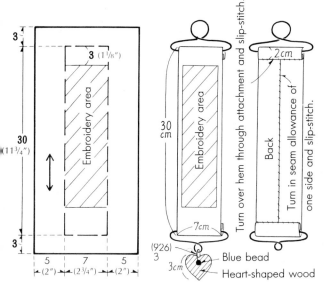

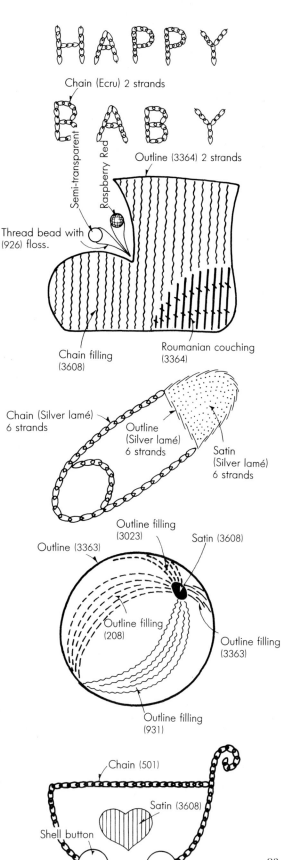

For a Newborn Baby

Instructions for Card on page 86, for Picture on
page 82 and for Bell Pull on page 83.

Card

Shown on page 84.

MATERIALS: Beige linen, 7 cm (2³/₄″) square. DMC six-strand embroidery floss, No. 25: Small amount each of Mauve (340), Almond Green (523), Antique Blue (931), Moss Green (3364) and Raspberry Red (3608). 3 Purple seed beads (1.7 mm or ¹/₁₆″). Blue cardboard, 27 cm by 12 cm (10⁵/₈″ × 4³/₄″). Matching envelope.
FINISHED SIZE: 12 cm by 9 cm (4³/₄″ × 3¹/₂″).

DIRECTIONS: Transfer design onto fabric and embroider. Cut out 6 cm × 6 cm from blue cardboard and fit in embroidered piece with glue.

How to Cut Blue Cardboard

Use 2 strands of floss unless otherwise directed.

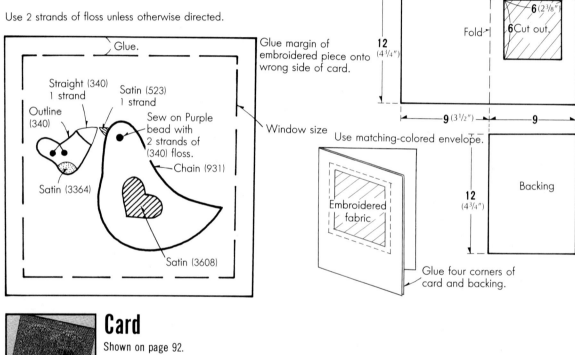

Glue margin of embroidered piece onto wrong side of card.

Glue.

Straight (340) 1 strand
Satin (523) 1 strand
Outline (340)
Sew on Purple bead with 2 strands of (340) floss.
Chain (931)
Satin (3364)
Satin (3608)

Window size

Use matching-colored envelope.

Embroidered fabric

Backing

Glue four corners of card and backing.

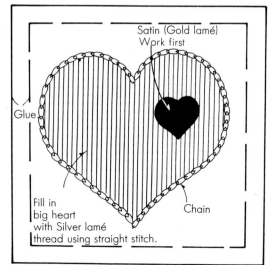

Card

Shown on page 92.

MATERIALS: Beige linen, 7 cm (2³/₄″) square. Gold and Silver lamé threads. Beige cardboard, 27 cm by 12 cm (10⁵/₈″ × 4³/₄″). Envelope in matching color.
FINISHED SIZE: 12 cm by 9 cm (4³/₄″ × 3¹/₂″).
DIRECTIONS: Transfer design onto fabric and start embroidering with small heart. Follow directions for above card.

Use 3 strands of floss unless otherwise directed.

Satin (Gold lamé) Work first

Glue

Fill in big heart with Silver lamé thread using straight stitch.

Chain

Pochette

Shown on page 89.

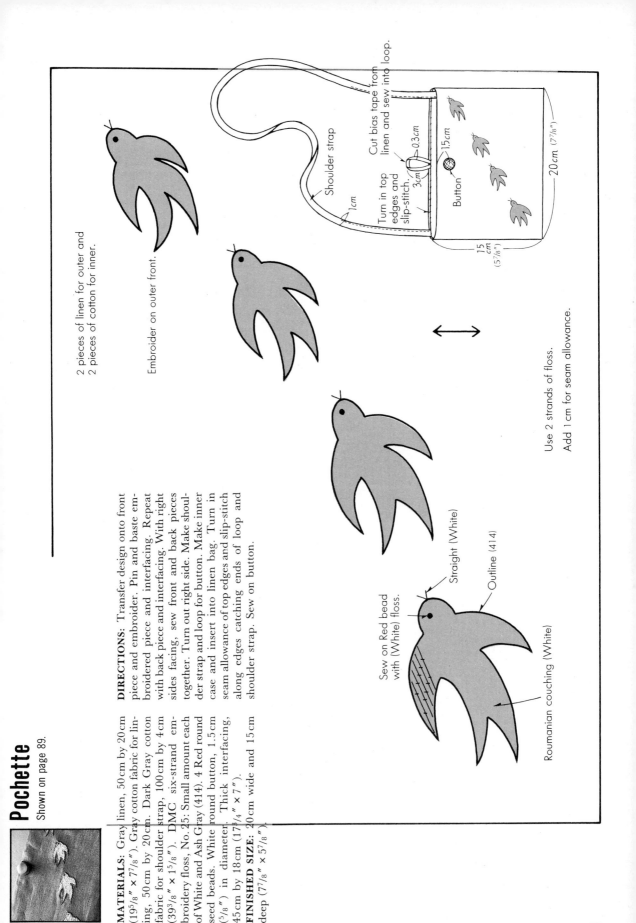

2 pieces of linen for outer and
2 pieces of cotton for inner.

Embroider on outer front.

Shoulder strap

Cut bias tape from linen and sew into loop.

Turn in top edges and slip-stitch.

0.3 cm

1 cm

3 cm

1.5 cm

Button

20 cm (7⅞")

15 cm (5⅞")

Use 2 strands of floss.

Add 1 cm for seam allowance.

Straight (White)

Outline (414)

Sew on Red bead with (White) floss.

Roumanian couching (White)

MATERIALS: Gray linen, 50 cm by 20 cm (19⅝" × 7⅞"). Gray cotton fabric for lining, 50 cm by 20 cm. Dark Gray cotton fabric for shoulder strap, 100 cm by 4 cm (39³⁄₈" × 1⅝"). DMC six-strand embroidery floss, No. 25: Small amount each of White and Ash Gray (414). 4 Red round seed beads. White round button, 1.5 cm (⅝") in diameter. Thick interfacing, 45 cm by 18 cm (17³⁄₄" × 7").
FINISHED SIZE: 20 cm wide and 15 cm deep (7⅞" × 5⅞").

DIRECTIONS: Transfer design onto front piece and embroider. Pin and baste embroidered piece and interfacing. Repeat with back piece and interfacing. With right sides facing, sew front and back pieces together. Turn out right side. Make shoulder strap and loop for button. Make inner case and insert into linen bag. Turn in seam allowance of top edges and slip-stitch along edges catching ends of loop and shoulder strap. Sew on button.

87

Pochette and Sweat Shirt

Instructions for Pochette on page 87 and
for Sweat Shirt on page 90.

Sweat Shirt

Shown on page 89.

MATERIALS: Purchased Green sweat shirt. DMC six-strand embroidery floss, No. 25: Small amount each of Moss Green (936), Golden Green (580, 581), Drab (611) and Beige (3022). Green and Yellow crayon dye.
DIRECTIONS: Transfer design onto front of shirt. Dye trees with Green and Yellow dye and embroider.

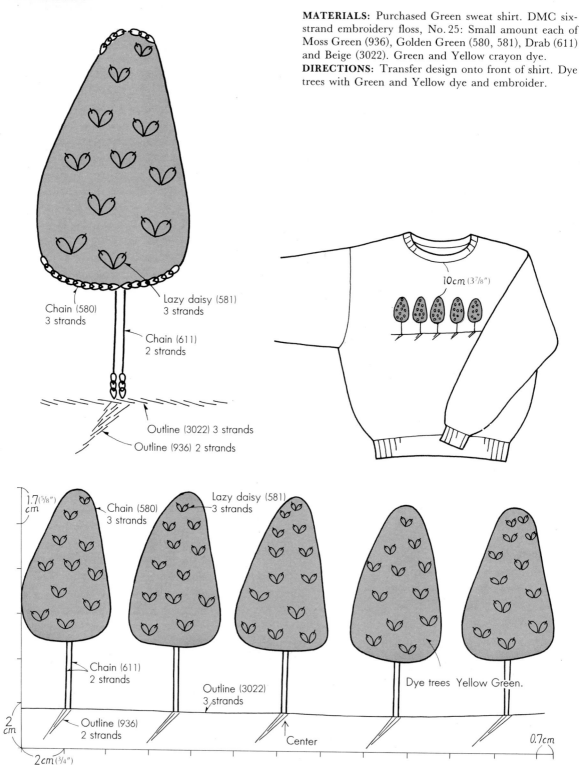

Chain (580)
3 strands

Lazy daisy (581)
3 strands

Chain (611)
2 strands

Outline (3022) 3 strands
Outline (936) 2 strands

10cm (3⅞")

1.7(⅝")
cm

Chain (580)
3 strands

Lazy daisy (581)
3 strands

Chain (611)
2 strands

Outline (3022)
3 strands

Outline (936)
2 strands

Dye trees Yellow Green.

Center

2
cm

2cm(¾")

0.7cm

Pillow Case

Shown on page 93.

MATERIALS: Gray cotton broadcloth, 52 cm by 176 cm (20½″ × 69¼″). DMC six-strand embroidery floss, No. 25: Small amount each of White, Ash Gray (415), Myrtle Gray (926), Beige (3022), Almond Green (502, 523) and Antique Blue (931).

FINISHED SIZE: 50 cm wide and 84 cm long (19⅝″ × 33⅛″).

DIRECTIONS: Transfer design onto fabric and embroider. Fold in half with right sides facing and sew side seams. Zigzag-stitch along raw edges. Turn out right side. Fold edge for opening twice and machine-stitch.

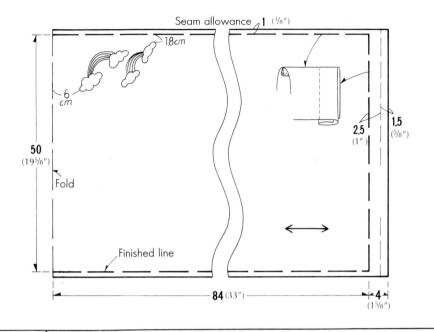

Seam allowance 1 (⅛″)

18 cm

6 cm

50 (19⅝″)

Fold

Finished line

2.5 (1″)

1.5 (⅝″)

84 (33″)

4 (1⅝″)

Finished line

Use 3 strands of floss unless otherwise directed.

Outline (931)

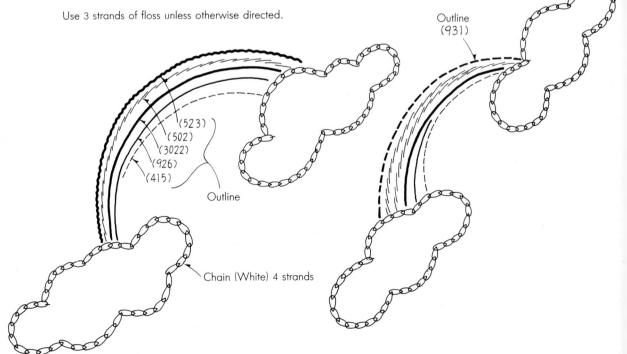

(523)
(502)
(3022)
(926)
(415)

Outline

Chain (White) 4 strands

91

For St. Valentine's Day

Instructions for Card on page 86, for Pillow on page 94, for Cosmetic Case on page 95 and for Pillow Case on page 91.

Pillow

Shown on page 93.

MATERIALS: Beige Brown linen, 55 cm by 27 cm ($21^5/_8'' \times 10^5/_8''$). DMC embroidery twist (Retors à broder): Small amount each of Beige Brown (2640), Olive Green (2520, 2580), Almond Green (2522) and Ecru. DMC six-strand embroidery floss, No. 25: Small amount each of Mauve (333), Cornflower Blue (792) and Smoke Gray (644). Wooden beads: 3 Brown and 1 Natural color, 0.7 cm ($^1/_4''$) in diameter; Light Brown, Natural and Blue, 2 each, 0.3 cm ($^1/_8''$) in diameter. 20 cm ($7^7/_8''$) long zipper. Inner pillow, 25 cm ($9^7/_8''$) square.

FINISHED SIZE: 25cm ($9^7/_8''$) square.

DIRECTIONS: Transfer design onto front and embroider. Sew on wooden beads. Sew zipper onto back. Sew top and botton seams and turn out right side. Insert inner pillow.

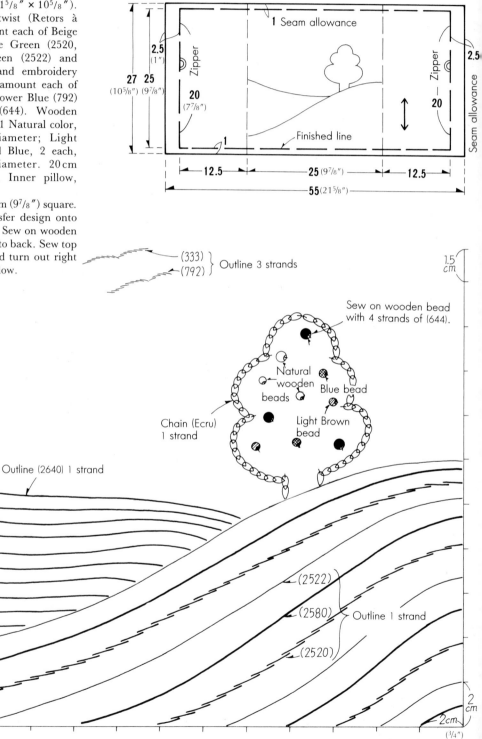

1 Seam allowance

Zipper

Finished line

Zipper

2.5 ($1''$)

27 ($10^5/_8''$) 25 ($9^7/_8''$)

20 ($7^7/_8''$)

20

2.5

Seam allowance

12.5 — 25 ($9^7/_8''$) — 12.5

55 ($21^5/_8''$)

(333) } Outline 3 strands
(792)

1.5 cm

Sew on wooden bead with 4 strands of (644).

Natural wooden beads

Blue bead

Chain (Ecru) 1 strand

Light Brown bead

Outline (2640) 1 strand

(2522)

(2580) Outline 1 strand

(2520)

1cm

2cm

2 cm ($^3/_4''$)

94

Cosmetic Case

Shown on page 93.

MATERIALS: Black linen, 70 cm by 25 cm (27½″ × 9⅞″). Black cotton satin for lining, 70 cm by 25 cm. DMC six-strand embroidery floss, No. 25: Small amount of Ash Gray (317). 34 Silver round seed beads (1.7 mm or ¹/₁₆″). 22 cm (8⅝″) long zipper. Black and White crayon dye.
FINISHED SIZE: See diagram.

DIRECTIONS: Cut fabric. Transfer design onto front piece. Color dog with Black and White crayon dye to make gray. Outline stitch all around dog and attach beads. Sew front, gusset and back together with right sides facing. Sew zipper along top edges. Make inner case in same manner and insert into outer case. Turn in seam allowance of top edges and slip-stitch along zipper tape.

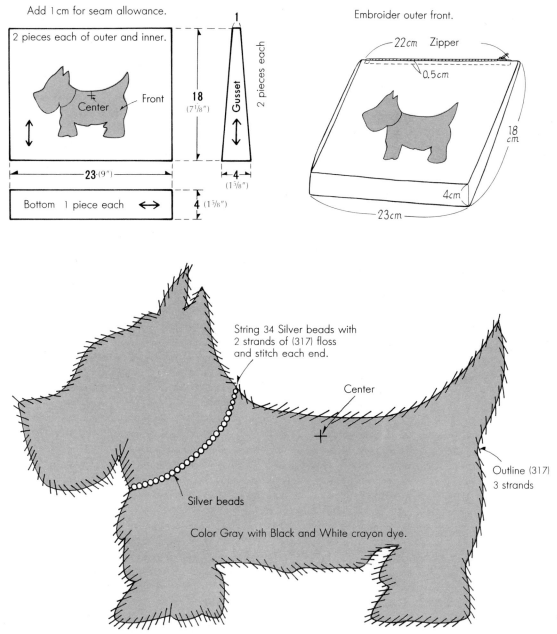

Add 1 cm for seam allowance.

2 pieces each of outer and inner.

Center Front

18 (7⅛″)

Gusset

2 pieces each

1

4 (1⅜″)

23·(9″)

Bottom 1 piece each

4 (1⅜″)

Embroider outer front.

22cm Zipper

0.5cm

18 cm

4cm

23cm

String 34 Silver beads with 2 strands of (317) floss and stitch each end.

Center

Silver beads

Outline (317) 3 strands

Color Gray with Black and White crayon dye.

Heartful of Gifts

Instructions for Picture on page 98,
for Pillow on page 118 and for
Cosmetic Case on page 114.

Picture

Shown on page 96.

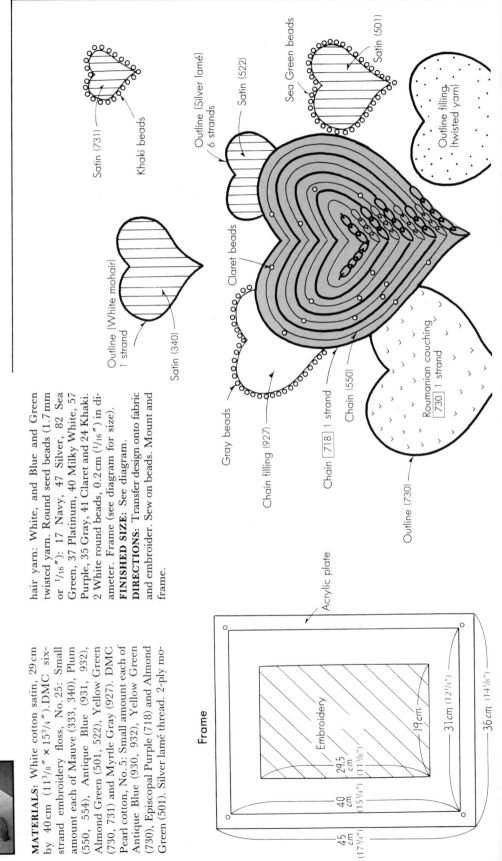

MATERIALS: White cotton satin, 29 cm by 40 cm (11³/₈″ × 15³/₄″). DMC six-strand embroidery floss, No. 25: Small amount each of Mauve (333, 340), (550, 554), Antique Blue (931, 932), Almond Green (501, 522), Yellow Green (730, 731) and Myrtle Gray (927). DMC Pearl cotton, No. 5: Small amount each of Antique Blue (930, 932), Yellow Green (730), Episcopal Purple (718) and Almond Green (501). Silver lamé thread. 2-ply mo-hair yarn: White, and Blue and Green twisted yarn. Round seed beads (1.7 mm or ¹/₁₆″): 17 Navy, 47 Silver, 82 Sea Green, 37 Platinum, 40 Milky White, 57 Purple, 35 Gray, 41 Claret and 24 Khaki. 2 White round beads, 0.2 cm (¹/₁₆″) in diameter. Frame (see diagram for size).

FINISHED SIZE: See diagram.

DIRECTIONS: Transfer design onto fabric and embroider. Sew on beads. Mount and frame.

Satin (731)

Khaki beads

Outline (Silver lamé) 6 strands

Satin (522)

Sea Green beads

Satin (501)

Outline filling (twisted yarn)

Outline (White mohair) 1 strand

Satin (340)

Claret beads

Gray beads

Chain filling (927)

Chain 718 1 strand

Chain (550)

Roumanian couching 730 1 strand

Outline (730)

Frame

Acrylic plate

Embroidery

19 cm

24.5 cm (11⁵/₈″)

40 cm (15³/₄″)

31 cm (12¹/₄″)

36 cm (14¹/₈″)

45 cm (17³/₄″)

98

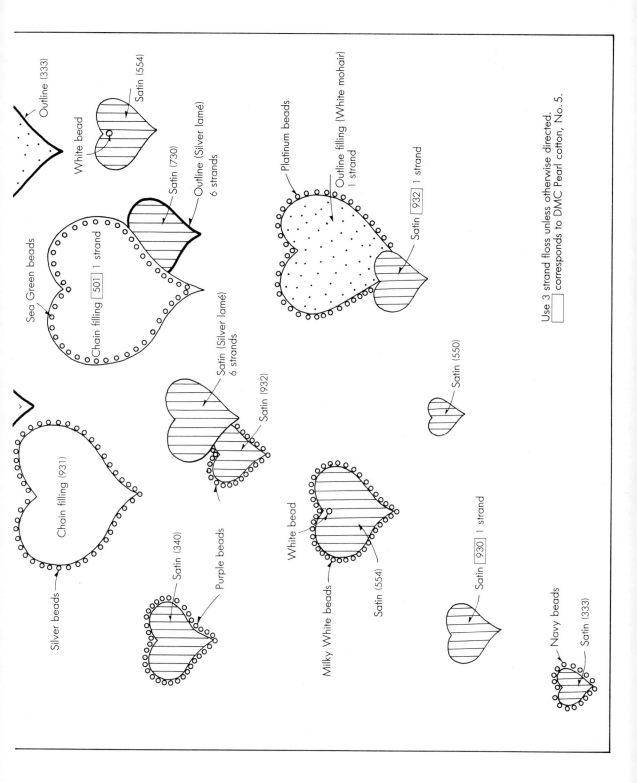

Outline (333)

White bead

Satin (554)

Satin (730)

Outline (Silver lamé)
6 strands

Sea Green beads

Chain filling 501 1 strand

Silver beads

Chain filling (931)

Satin (340)

Purple beads

Satin (Silver lamé)
6 strands

Satin (932)

White bead

Milky White beads

Satin (554)

Platinum beads

Outline filling (White mohair)
1 strand

Satin 932 1 strand

Satin (550)

Satin 930 1 strand

Navy beads

Satin (333)

Use 3 strand floss unless otherwise directed.
☐ corresponds to DMC Pearl cotton, No. 5.

99

Photo Frames and Table Center

Instructions for Frames on page 102 and for
Table Center on page 74.

Photo Frames

Shown on page 100.

MATERIALS: Blue linen, 40 cm by 20 cm (15³/₄″ × 7⁷/₈″) for *Rectangular Frame*. Light-weight Blue Green denim, 25 cm by 13 cm (9⁷/₈″ × 5¹/₈″) for *Square Frame*. DMC six-strand embroidery floss, No. 25: Small amount each of Mauve (340), Plum (553), Almond Green (502), Golden Green (580), Yellow Green (733), Umber (739) and White. Silver lamé thread. Round seed beads (1.7 mm or ¹/₁₆″):

56 Platinum for *Rectangular Frame*; 40 Navy and 8 Platinum for *Square Frame*. Frame: 12 cm by 16.5 cm (4³/₄″ × 6¹/₂″) and 9 cm (3¹/₂″) square. Blue satin ribbon, 1 cm by 30 cm (³/₈″ × 11³/₄″). Glue.

FINISHED SIZE: Same size as frames.

DIRECTIONS: Transfer design onto fabric and embroider. Make frames following diagrams on opposite page.

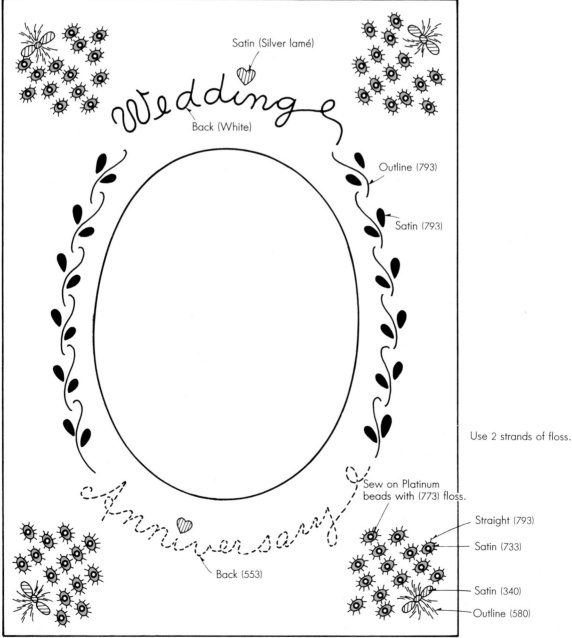

Satin (Silver lamé)

Back (White)

Outline (793)

Satin (793)

Use 2 strands of floss.

Sew on Platinum beads with (773) floss.

Straight (793)

Satin (733)

Back (553)

Satin (340)

Outline (580)

Rectangular Frame

① ← 12.5 (4⅞") →
1.5
Transfer design onto fabric and embroider.
17 (6¾")
Clip into margin along oval cut-out.
1.5 (⅝")
Glue.

Round off edges of urethane foam and place on the cardboard.
Cover with embroidered piece and glue.

② ← 12 (4¾") →
0.5
Cut back piece same size as front.
Glue to wrong side of cardboard.
Glue paper on top showing 0.5cm (¼") fabric.
16.5 (6½")
0.5

③ Stand
Glue.
1.2
2 (¼")
1.2
Glue fabric onto cardboard for stand.
0.2 cm (1/16")
1.2
Insert end of ribbon between front and back pieces.

④ 2cm
Glue ribbon onto top.
11 cm
Cover back surface with fabric.

Make a slit in back piece, insert top of stand and glue.

Square Frame

① ← 9.5 (3¾") →
1 (⅜")
Embroider.
9.5
Clip into margin at corners, turn margin to back and glue.
1

Follow directions for Rectangular Frame.

② ← 9 (3½") →
0.5 (¼")
Glue back piece onto cardboard and glue paper on top.
9
0.5

③ Fold ribbon in half lengthwise and stitch. Glue ends of ribbon between front and back pieces.
2.5 cm
9 cm
Open side
Glue front and back together along three sides leaving one side open.
9cm (3½")

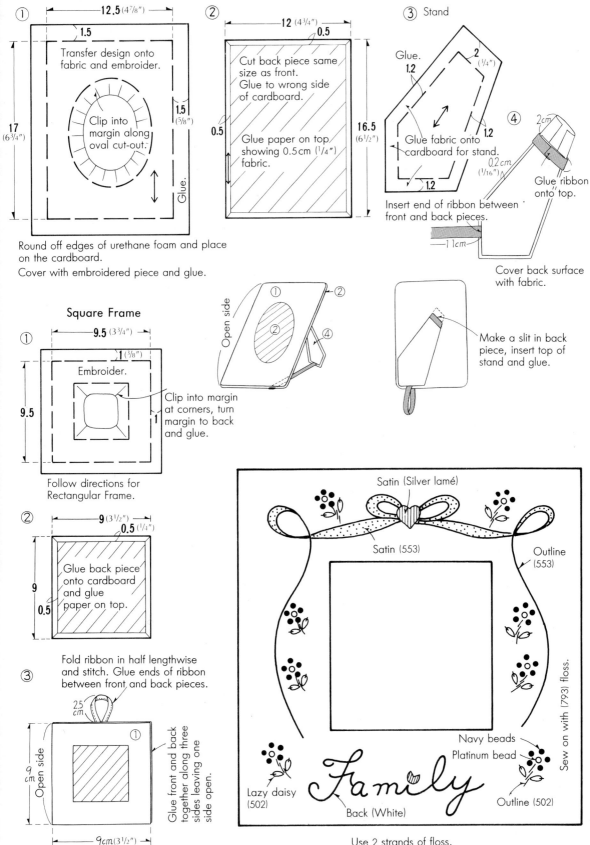

Satin (Silver lamé)
Satin (553)
Outline (553)
Sew on with (793) floss.
Navy beads
Platinum bead
Outline (502)
Family
Back (White)
Lazy daisy (502)

Use 2 strands of floss.

103

Merry Christmas

Instructions for Xmas Card and Brooches
on page 106, and for Sweater and
Table Center on page 107.

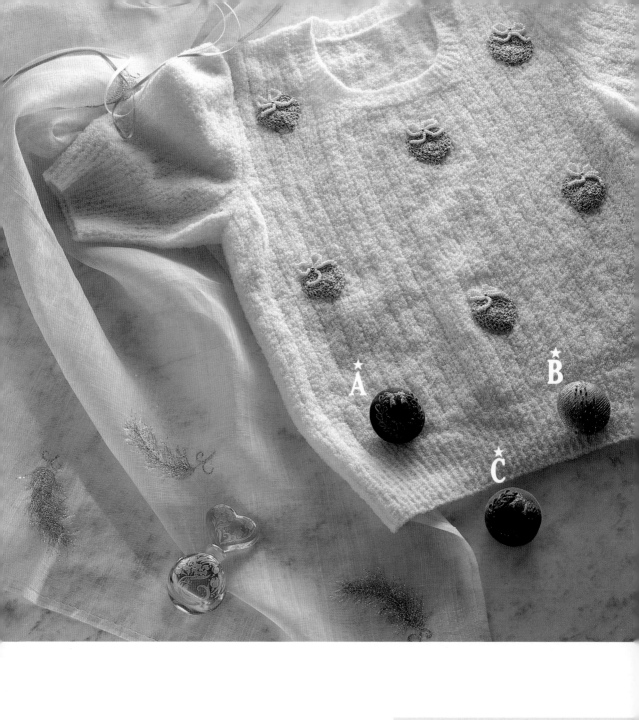

Xmas Card

Shown on page 104.

MATERIALS: Moss Green linen, 7 cm (2³/₄″) square.
DMC six-strand embroidery floss, No. 25: Small amount
of Scarlet (304). Gold lamé thread. Ball-shaped Red wood
bead, 0.6 cm (¹/₄″) in diameter. Star-shaped Gold spangle, 0.5 cm (¹/₄″) wide. Olive Green cardboard, 27 cm by
12 cm (10⁵/₈″ × 4³/₄″). Envelope.
FINISHED SIZE: 12 cm by 9 cm (4³/₄″ × 3¹/₂″).
DIRECTIONS: Transfer design onto fabric and embroider. Attach bead and glue spangle. See directions for card
shown on page 86.

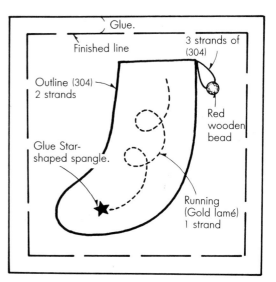

Brooches

Shown on page 105.

MATERIALS: Velveteen:
Moss Green for *A* and
Light Brown for *C*, 7 cm
(2³/₄″) square each. Gold
lamé fabric, 7 cm square for
B. Cotton satin in matching color for lining, 6 cm
(2³/₈″) square each. DMC
six-strand embroidery floss,
No. 25: Small amount each
of Drab (610), Episcopal
Purple (915) and Gold lamé
thread for *A*; Beige (3023)
and Gold lamé thread for
B; Moss Green (937), Episcopal Purple (915) and
Gold lamé thread for *C*.
Round seed beads (1.7 mm
or ¹/₁₆″): Dark Red, 25
pieces each for *A* and *C*; 13
Bronze and 11 Pearl Gray
for *B*. Cardboard, 4 cm
(1⁵/₈″) in diameter. Cot-
ton. Safety pins.
FINISHED SIZE: 4 cm (1⁵/₈″) in diameter.
DIRECTIONS: Transfer design onto fabric
and embroider. Make brooches following instructions on page 3.

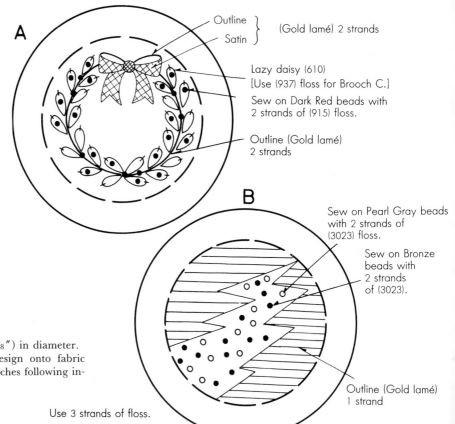

Use 3 strands of floss.

Sweater

Shown on page 105.

MATERIALS: Purchased Off-White sweater. DMC six-strand embroidery floss, No. 25: Small amount of Ecru. Gold lamé thread (same thickness as baby yarn). 6 ball-shaped Gold beads, 0.3 cm (1/8″) in diameter. 312 pearl beads, 0.3 cm in diameter.

DIRECTIONS: Transfer design onto sweater and embroider with Gold lamé thread. Sew on Gold beads. Shape threaded pearl beads into bow and sew on. See page 80 for arrangement.

See page 80 for arrangement.

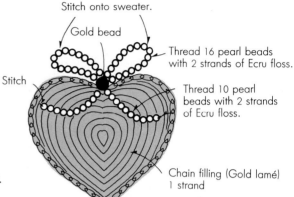

Stitch onto sweater.

Gold bead

Thread 16 pearl beads with 2 strands of Ecru floss.

Stitch

Thread 10 pearl beads with 2 strands of Ecru floss.

Chain filling (Gold lamé) 1 strand

Table Center

Shown on page 105.

MATERIALS: Beige pina cloth, 78 cm (30³/4″) square. Small amount each of Silver and Gold lamé threads.
FINISHED SIZE: 75 cm (29¹/2″) square.
DIRECTIONS: Fold edges twice and slip-stitch. Transfer design onto fabric and embroider.

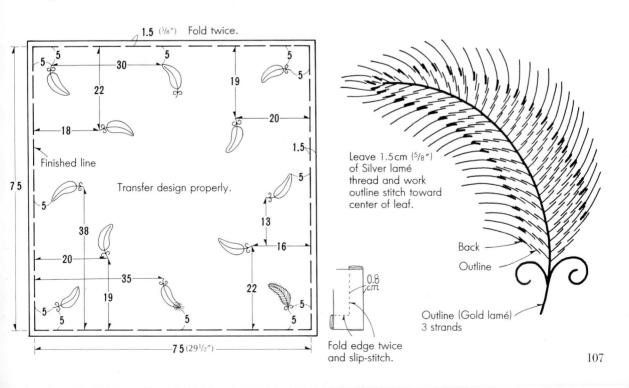

1.5 (5/8″) Fold twice.

5   5   30   5   5   5   19   5

22

18   20

Finished line   1.5

7 5   Transfer design properly.   5

5   3

38   13

20   16

35   22

19   5

5   5   5   5

7 5 (29¹/2″)

Fold edge twice and slip-stitch.

0.8 cm

Leave 1.5 cm (5/8″) of Silver lamé thread and work outline stitch toward center of leaf.

Back

Outline

Outline (Gold lamé) 3 strands

Merry Christmas

Instructions for Coasters on
page 110 and for Mats
on page 76.

Coasters

Shown on page 108.

Use 2 strand floss.

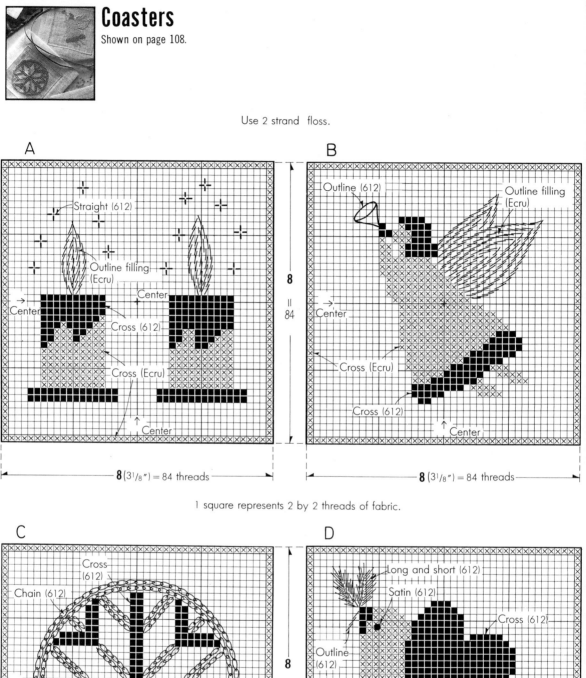

A

Straight (612)

Outline filling (Ecru)

Center

Center

Cross (612)

Cross (Ecru)

Center

$8 = 84$

$8 (3^1/_8") = 84$ threads

B

Outline (612)

Outline filling (Ecru)

Center

Center

Cross (Ecru)

Cross (612)

Center

$8 (3^1/_8") = 84$ threads

1 square represents 2 by 2 threads of fabric.

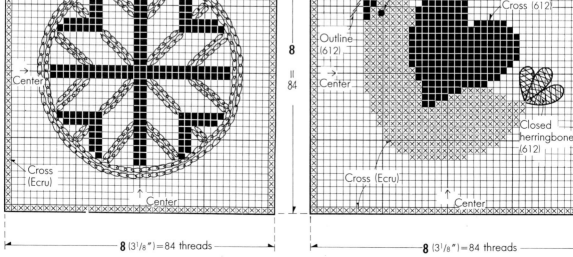

C

Cross (612)

Chain (612)

Center

Cross (Ecru)

Center

$8 = 84$

$8 (3^1/_8") = 84$ threads

D

Long and short (612)

Satin (612)

Cross (612)

Outline (612)

Center

Closed herringbone (612)

Cross (Ecru)

Center

$8 (3^1/_8") = 84$ threads

MATERIALS for 6 coasters: Off-White linen (10.8 threads per 10cm), 108cm by 18cm (42½″ × 7″). DMC six-strand embroidery floss, No. 25: 1½ skeins of Ecru and ½ skein of Drab (612).

FINISHED SIZE: 12cm (4¾″) square.

DIRECTIONS: Cut linen into 18cm (7″) square. Mark center and embroider following chart. Fold edges twice and slip-stitch.

Cut linen into 18cm square.

Fold twice and slip-stitch.

Embroider

21 threads = 2)

84 threads

8

2 = 21 threads)

12 (4¾″) = 126 threads

Closed Herringbone Stitch

out 3

in 2

1 out

5 out 4 in

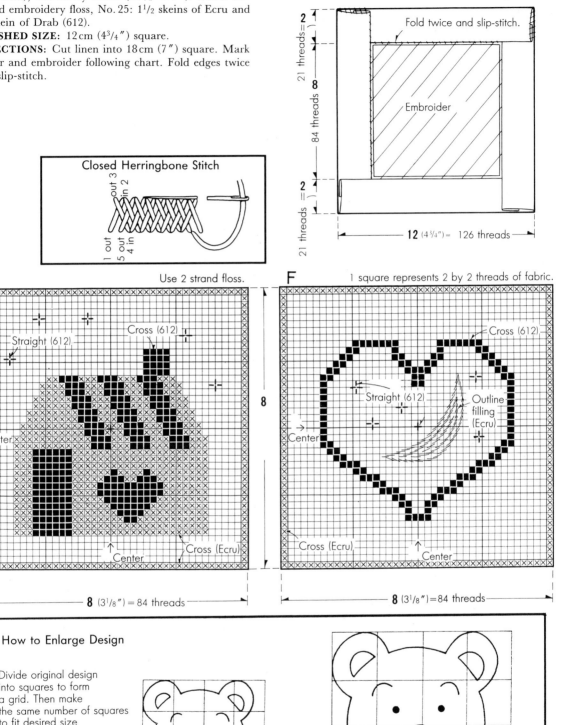

E   Use 2 strand floss.

Straight (612)

Cross (612)

Center

Center

Cross (Ecru)

8 (3⅛″) = 84 threads

8

F   1 square represents 2 by 2 threads of fabric.

Cross (612)

Straight (612)

Outline filling (Ecru)

Center

Cross (Ecru)

Center

8 (3⅛″) = 84 threads

How to Enlarge Design

Divide original design into squares to form a grid. Then make the same number of squares to fit desired size of design. Copy design from smaller squares.

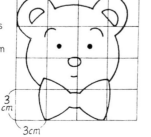

3 cm

3cm

0 1 2 3 4 5 6 7 8 9 10 11 12 13

Christmas Ornament

Instructions on page 113.

Christmas Ornament

Shown on page 112.

MATERIALS: White banana cloth or White lawn, 6 pieces each of 10 cm (3⅞″) square. DMC six-strand embroidery floss, No. 25: Small amount each of Ecru and Smoke Gray (644, 822). Silver and Gold lamé threads. 31 White round beads, 0.2 cm (1/16″) in diameter. Frame (see diagram for size).

FINISHED SIZE: See diagram.

DIRECTIONS: Transfer design onto 10 cm (3⅞″) square lawn and embroider. Cut off excess fabric 0.3 cm (⅛″) beyond outline. Fit in frame.

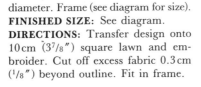

33 cm

Bow

Star   Tree

Bell   Angel   Candles

8.5 cm (3⅜″) in diameter

33 cm (13″)

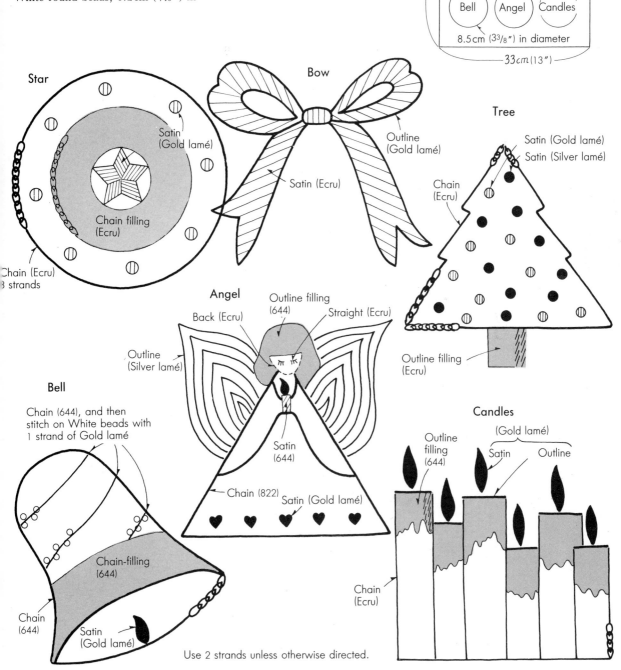

Star

Satin (Gold lamé)

Chain filling (Ecru)

Chain (Ecru) 3 strands

Bow

Outline (Gold lamé)

Satin (Ecru)

Tree

Satin (Gold lamé)
Satin (Silver lamé)

Chain (Ecru)

Outline filling (Ecru)

Angel

Outline filling (644)

Back (Ecru)   Straight (Ecru)

Outline (Silver lamé)

Satin (644)

Chain (822)   Satin (Gold lamé)

Bell

Chain (644), and then stitch on White beads with 1 strand of Gold lamé

Chain-filling (644)

Chain (644)

Satin (Gold lamé)

Candles

(Gold lamé)

Outline filling (644)   Satin   Outline

Chain (Ecru)

Use 2 strands unless otherwise directed.

113

Cosmetic Case

Shown on page 97.

MATERIALS: Moss Green linen, 70 cm by 23 cm (27½″ × 9″). Smoke Green cotton fabric for lining, 70 cm by 23 cm. DMC six-strand embroidery floss, No. 25: Small amount each of Sage Green (520, 522), Moss Green (3363), Myrtle Gray (927). Silver lamé thread. 20 cm (7⅞″) long zipper.

FINISHED SIZE: 24 cm by 18 cm (9½″ × 7″).

DIRECTIONS: Transfer design onto front piece and embroider. Sew front, gusset and back together. Sew zipper along top edge. Make inner case. Insert inner case into outer one, turn in seam allowance and slip-stitch onto zipper tape.

2 Seam allowance

Finished line

Center

2 pieces each of outer and inner

Fold.

Bottom

18 (7⅛″)

3

1

1

24 (10″)

2 pieces each of outer and inner

Gusset

18

4

1

Sew zipper along top edge.

Turn in seam allowance of inner case and slip-stich.

Sew gusset onto front and back.

Sew bottom seam and press seam open.

20 cm Zipper

18 cm

Sew inner case in same manner.

24 cm

4 cm (1⅝″)

Satin (927) 2 strands

Satin (522) 2 strands

Chain (520)

Outline (3363) 2 strands

Outline (927)

Center

Satin (Silver lamé)

machi

Use 3 strands unless otherwise directed.

Pillow

Shown on page 97.

MATERIALS: Gray linen, 64 cm by 33 cm (25 1/4″ × 12 1/4″). DMC six-strand embroidery floss, No. 25: Small amount each of Ecru, Green (3052), Sage Green (523), Beige (3023) and Episcopal Purple (917). 31 Platinum round seed beads (1.7 mm or 1/16″). 27 cm (10 5/8″) long zipper. Inner pillow, 30 cm (11 3/4″) square.

FINISHED SIZE: 30 cm (11 3/4″) square.

DIRECTIONS: Transfer design onto fabric and embroider. Make pillow according to diagrams.

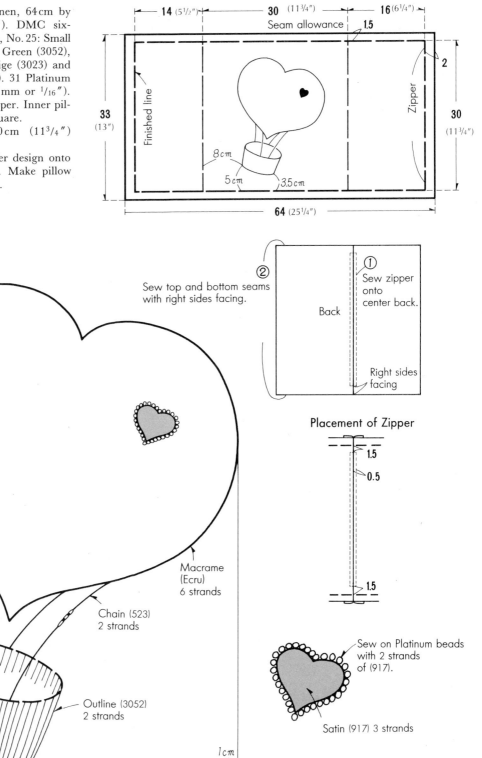

14 (5 1/2″)   30 (11 3/4″)   16 (6 1/4″)

Seam allowance   1.5

Finished line

Zipper

2

33 (13″)   30 (11 3/4″)

8 cm   5 cm   3.5 cm

64 (25 1/4″)

② Sew top and bottom seams with right sides facing.

① Sew zipper onto center back.

Back

Right sides facing

Placement of Zipper

1.5
0.5
1.5

1 cm

Macrame (Ecru) 6 strands

Chain (3023) 3 strands

Chain (523) 2 strands

Outline (3052) 2 strands

2 cm
2 cm

1 cm

Sew on Platinum beads with 2 strands of (917).

Satin (917) 3 strands

115